NCERT MCQs

Indian Economy

Class 9-12 (Old+New)

Author
Ameebh Ranjan
Series Editor
Surya Singh

arihant
SUCCESS AND NOTHING LESS

arihant
SUCCESS AND NOTHING LESS

ARIHANT PUBLICATIONS (INDIA) LIMITED

Administrative & Production Offices

Regd. Office

'Ramchhaya' 4577/15, Agarwal Road, Darya Ganj, New Delhi -110002
Tele: 011- 47630600, 43518550

Head Office

Kalindi, TP Nagar, Meerut (UP) - 250002
Tel: 0121-7156203, 7156204

Sales & Support Offices

Agra, Ahmedabad, Bengaluru, Bareilly, Chennai, Delhi, Guwahati, Hyderabad, Jaipur, Jhansi, Kolkata, Lucknow, Nagpur & Pune.

PRICE ₹90.00

PO No : TXT-59-T059114-5-24

Published by Arihant Publications (India) Ltd.

For further information about the books published by Arihant, log on to www.arihantbooks.com or e-mail at info@arihantbooks.com

Follow us on

Few Words

NCERTs are the Foundation in the Journey of IAS...

Civil Service Examinations are the most prestigious, tough and challenging examinations in India.

Being the toughest exam, it automatically consists of a vast and a detailed syllabus. Aspirants often find it difficult to cover the entire syllabus and lack a right direction for a proper and a systematic study for the exam.

The most important aspect of this preparation journey are the NCERT books. Every year approximately **35-40 questions** directly or indirectly asked from NCERT books.

NCERT books also play a key role in understanding the Basic Concepts; so that aspirants can easily form the basic foundation of the entire syllabus. But due to the demand for many NCERT books which are required for study, it becomes exhausting to cover each and every NCERT book.

NCERT MCQs series presented by Arihant Publications covers MCQs from Class 6th to 12th NCERT books (both Old & New) in a comprehensive manner.

Features of Revised Edition

- Each and Every Question is designed as per Latest Pattern of UPSC and State PCS.
- The chapter-wise questions given in the sequential form in the series along with the source of the questions.
- 100% Error free and detailed explanations will make the preparation easy and convenient.
- Additional coverage of Tamil Nadu Board and NIOS Books.
- 3 Practice Sets also provided for overall practice related to subject.

The book is adorned with questions prepared by a team of experts along with a vital role played by the Project Management team with members: Mona Yadav (Project Manager), Manshi Gupta (Project Coordinator), Seema Saini (Proof Reading TL), Pradeep Chaudhary (DTP TL), Bilal and Ankit Tyagi (Cover and Inner designer).

We hope this book will help the aspirants to achieve their goals of clearing UPSC as well as State PCS exams. Your valuable suggestions have always inspired us to strive for useful, authentic and more trustworthy publications.
So your inputs and suggestions are welcomed for subsequent editions.

We wish you all the very best for your preparation and journey!!

Authors

CONTENTS

Chapter 01

Economy : An Introduction

Economy : An Introduction

Economics

Introduction

- Economic activities are carried out in the form of investment, production and consumption

Types

On the basis of Ownership and Management of Resources

- Capitalist Economy (United States of America, United Kingdom)
- Socialist Economy (Russia ,China)
- Mixed Economy (India)

On the basis of Development

- Developed Economy (France, Japan)
- Developing Economy (India, China)
- Less Developed Economy (Bangladesh, South Sudan)

On the Basis of Trade

- Open economy India, Chille, Argentina
- Closed Economy India (before 1991)

Branches of Economics

- **Macro Economics** National Income, Poverty, Employment etc.
- **Micro Economics** Price Discrimination, Individual Income

Features of Indian Economy

Traditional Features

- Low Per Capita Income
- Unemployment

Modern Features

- Planned Economy
- Industrial Development

Economic Development

Human Development Index (HDI)

- Introduced by UNDP in 1990

Dimensions of HDI

- Life Expectancy Index
- Educational Attainment Index
- Standard of living Index

Multi-Dimensional Poverty Index MPI

- Launched by UNDP and OPHI in 2010
- **Indicators** Education, Health, Standard of Living

World Happiness Report (WHR)

- First coined by the King of Bhutan in 1972
- **Indicators** Social Support, Health Life Expectancy at Birth, Absence of Corruption

Gender Inequality Index (GII)

- Measure Gender Inequality
- **Indicators** Reproduction, Health, Empowerment, Economic Status

Global Hunger Index (GHI)

- Published annually by concern Worldwide and welthungerhilfe
- **Indicators** Under Nourishment, Child Wasting, Child Stunting, Child Mortality

Human Capital, Human Development and Sustainable Development

Human Capital

- Population becomes Human Capital
- Considered Education and health as a means to increase Labour Productivity
- Stock of Skill and Productive Knowledge
- Investment in Education is one of the main Sources

Human Development

- Based on the Education, Health is integral part of Human being
- People have the ability to read and write alongwith the ability to lead a long and healthy life

Economic Growth

- Increase in production of Goods and Service in an Economy
- Quantitative Concept

Sustainable Development

- The Development to achieve the needs of Present Generation
- Ensures the well-being of Individuals
- Sustainable Development Goals (SDGs) was set up in 2015 by United Nations General Assembly
- Ensures healthy life and promote well-being

SOURCE **New NCERT Class IX** *(The Story of Village Palampur)*, **New NCERT Class IX** *(People as a Resource)*, **Old NCERT Class IX & X** *(An Overview of the Indian Economy)*, **New NCERT Class X** *(Sectors of the Indian Economy)*, **New NCERT Class X** *(Development)*, **New NCERT Class XI** *(Indian Economy 1950-1990)*, **New NCERT Class XI** *(Indian Economy on the Eve of Independence)*, **New NCERT Class XI** *(Human Capital Formation in India)*, **New NCERT Class XI** *(Environment and Sustainable Development)*, **New NCERT Class XII** *(Introduction)*, **Tamil Nadu Board Class XI** *(Introduction to Micro Economics)*

Basic of Economy

1 Consider the following characteristics of an economy on the basis of Development. *(Chap 1, Class-XI, New NCERT)*

1. Developed economy has advanced technological infrastructure and diverse industrial and service sectors.
2. Developing economy has a low socio-economic indicators and Moderate Human Development Index.
3. Less developed economy exhibit the lowest indicators of socio-economic development.

Which of the statements given above is/are correct?

(a) Only 1 (b) 1 and 2
(c) 2 and 3 (d) 1, 2 and 3

Ans. (d)

Exp. All the statements given above are correct *wrt* characteristics of an economy on the basis of Development.

Countries with relatively high levels of economic growth are considered to have developed economy. While a developing country is a country with a relatively low standard of living, undeveloped industrial base, and moderate the low Human Development Index (HDI).

This index is a comparative measure of poverty, literacy, education, life expectancy and other factors for countries world wide.

Less developed economy or sometimes referred to Least Developed Countries (LDCs) are low income countries and face challenges to Sustainable development.

2 With reference to the Ownership and Management of Resources. Which of the following statements is incorrect? *(Chap 1, Class-XI, Tamil Nadu Board)*

(a) Economies can be classified into Capitalist, Socialist and Mixed economy.
(b) In Capital economy, the private enterprise are the main spheres of production and control the production of price.
(c) In Socialist economy, characterised by social ownership, government decides on the products and services in line with society requirements.
(d) In Mixed economy, organised with some socialistic elements but maintain private ownership of the means of production.

Ans. (d)

Exp. Statement (d) is incorrect with reference to the Ownership and Management of Resources because in mixed economy, the means of production are held by both private companies and public or state ownership.

A mixed economy combines the best features of capitalism and socialism. Thus mixed economy has some elements of both free enterprise or capitalist economy as well as a government controlled socialist economy.

3 Which of the following statements is not true about the Indian economy? *(Chap 1, Class-XI, Tamil Nadu Board)*

(a) Its share of world population is 16% but its share of world GDP is only 1.6%.
(b) The share of services sector in India's GDP is only 25%.
(c) 58% of its working population is engaged in agriculture, but the contribution of agriculture to the national income is 22%.
(d) India occupies only 2.4% of the world's geographical

Ans. (b)

Exp. Statement (b) is not true about the Indian economy as the share of services sector in India's GDP in 2009-2010 was 57.09% and in 2012-2013 was 59.29%.

As per the Economic Survey 2022-2023, the share of services in GVA at current basic prices is 53.4% in 2022-2023 (1st AE).

4 Consider the following statements. *(Chap 1, Class-XII, New NCERT)*

1. Adam Smith was a Scottish economist and regarded as 'Father of Modern Economics'.
2. He wrote two classic works, the Theory of Moral Sentiments (1759) and an inquiry into the nature and causes of the Wealth of Nations (1776).

Which of the statement(s) given above is/are correct?

(a) Only 1 (b) Only 2
(c) Both 1 and 2 (d) Neither 1 nor 2

Ans. (c)

Exp. Both statements (1) and (2) are correct.

Adam Smith was a Scottish economist and regarded as 'Father of Modern Economics'. His work include the Theory of Moral Sentiments (1759) and an inquiry into the nature and causes of the Wealth of Nation in 1776. His work is regarded as the first major comprehensive book on the subject. It is a fundamental work in classical economies, which deals with topics of division of labour, productivity and free markets.

5 With regard to the difference between micro and macro economics, which of the following statement(s) is/are correct? *(Chap 1, Class-XII, New NCERT)*

1. In macro economics, aggregate output of goods and services at the level of nation is measured whereas in micro economics, individual factors of production are studied.
2. Macro economic policies are pursued by the state itself or statutory bodies like the Reserve Bank of India (RBI) whereas policies concerning micro economics are pursued by individual agents only.

Select the correct answer using the codes given below.

(a) Only 1 (b) Only 2
(c) Both 1 and 2 (d) Neither 1 nor 2

Ans. (a)

Exp. Statement (1) is correct with regard to the difference between micro and macro economics as in macroeconomics, the aggregate output of goods and services, employment level, price level, etc are measured at the level of nation whereas microeconomics focuses on issues that affect individuals and companies.

However, both are interrelated and interdependent as macroeconomics takes into account various interlinkages, which may exist between different sectors of the economy.

Statement (2) is incorrect as other than economic decision taken by individual agents (such as household or automobile company), the action of entire sector such as automobile industry are also studied in microeconomics. It is also governed by state and the regulatory bodies like RBI.

6 **Consider the following statements.** *(Chap 1, Class-XII, Tamil Nadu Board)*

1. J M Keynes, was an English economist changed the theory and practice of macro economics.
2. He wrote 'The General Theory of Employment Interest and Money (1936)'.
3. He explained about fallout from Great Depression, when goods remained unsold and worker unemployed.

How many of the statements given above is/are correct?

(a) Only one (b) Only two
(c) All three (d) None of these

Ans. (c)

Exp. All three statements i.e., (1), (2) and (3) are correct regarding J M Keynes as he was an English economist whose ideas fundamentally changed the theory and practice of macroeconomics and the economic policies of governments. His ideas are fundamental to mainstream macroeconomics. He is known as the father of macroeconomics. Keynes advocated the use of fiscal and monetary policies to mitigate the adverse effects of economics recessions and depression. He detailed these ideas in his book 'The General Theory of Employment Interest and Money' which is published in 1936.

7 **Consider the following characteristics of a mixed economy.** *(Chap 2, Class-XII, New NCERT)*

1. The private and public sectors co-exist. Economic activity is directed by the government.
2. It promotes some form of regulation to protect the public, the environment or the interest of the state.

Which of the statement(s) given above is/are correct?

(a) Only 1 (b) Only 2
(c) Both 1 and 2 (d) Neither 1 nor 2

Ans. (c)

Exp. Both statements (1) and (2) are characteristics of a mixed economy as mixed economy means an economy where there is co-existence of public sector along with private sector.

A mixed economy is an economic system that combines elements of a capitalist, market based system, with a socialist, command economy system. It mixed elements such as private property rights, free trade, and privatisation, with socialist element such as regulation, the welfare state and re-distribution.

8 **With reference to the types of economies, which of the following statements is incorrect?** *(Chap 1, Class-XII, New NCERT)*

(a) In a centrally planned economy, the government or the central authority plans all the important activities in the economy.
(b) In a market economy, the central problems regarding how much and what to produce are solved through the coordination of economic activities brought about by the price signal.
(c) In a mixed economy, society has no private property since everything is owned by the state.
(d) In capitalist economy, purchasing power determines production and distribution of goods.

Ans. (c)

Exp. Statement (c) is incorrect with reference to the types of economies.

In a mixed economy, all the important decisions regarding production, distribution and consumption of goods and services are taken jointly by the government and the private sector. The right of private property is protected under mixed economy and the complete state ownership of all the resources is a characteristic of the communist economy.

9 **Consider the following characteristics of an economy.** *(Chap 1, Class-XII, New NCERT)*

1. There is private ownership of means of production.
2. Production takes place for selling the output in the market.
3. There is sale and purchase of labour services at a price, which is called the wage rate.

Which of the following types of economies is represented by the above characteristics?

(a) Capitalist Economy (b) Socialist Economy
(c) Mixed Economy (d) All of these

Ans. (a)

Exp. All the characteristics given above represent the capital economy. Capitalist economy is a type of economy that is represented by given characteristics.

In a capitalist economy, there is private ownership of means of production and are driven by the motive of profit-making. Production takes place for selling the output in the market.

In such economy, there is sale and purchase of labour services at a price which is called the wage rate (the labour that is sold and purchased against wages is referred to as 'wage labour'). Other characteristics of capitalist economy is minimal or no intervention of state, free market and Laissez Faire.

10 With reference to closed economy, which of the following statements is/are correct?

(Chap 1, Class-XII, New NCERT)

1. It means no import come into the country and no export leave it.
2. All goods and services are produced within the boundaries of a single economy.
3. It grows faster than open economics.
4. Its goal is to provide foreign consumers with everything they need.

How many of the statements given above is/are correct?

(a) Only one (b) Only two
(c) Only three (d) All four

Ans. (b)

Exp. Only two statements i.e., (1) and (2) are correct with respect to closed economy.

Closed economy is an economy in which neither export nor import takes place as no activity is conducted with other economies.

It is self-sufficient, where no imports are brought in and no exports are sent out. The goal is to provide consumers with everything that they need from within the economy.

Statements (3) and (4) are incorrect.

In closed economy it grows slower than open economy because they exclusively consume items created within their own country. External trade is negligible in closed economy.

11 The working of the price mechanism in a free-market economy refers to which one of the following? *(Chap 2, Class-XII, New NCERT)*

(a) The interplay of the forces of demand and supply
(b) Determination of the inflation rate in the economy
(c) Determination of the economy's propensity to consume
(d) Determination of the economy's full employment output

Ans. (a)

Exp. The working of the price mechanism in a free-market economy refers to the interplay of the forces of demand and supply. In the market economy (or capitalist economy) only those consumer goods are produced that are in demand. Purchasing power is the main determinant of production, consumption and distribution of goods in a free-market economy.

Sectors of Indian Economy

12 Which of the following is the correct increasing order of the contribution of the three sectors to the GDP of India? *(Chap 2, Class-X, New NCERT)*

(a) Agriculture < Service < Industry
(b) Agriculture < Industry < Service
(c) Service < Industry < Agriculture
(d) Industry < Agriculture < Service

Ans. (b)

Exp. The correct increasing order of the contribution of the three sectors to the GDP of India is Agriculture < Industry < Service.

Gross Domestic Product (GDP) is the value of all final goods and services produced within a country during a particular financial year. According to RBI's 2021 estimates, the contribution of agriculture, industry and service sector in Indian GDP is 20.19%, 25.92% and 53.89% respectively.

13 Which of the following statements is correct regarding public and private sectors?

(Chap 2, Class-X, New NCERT)

1. In public sector, organisation controlled and managed by the government, either fully or partially.
2. Private sector entities are owned by individuals with no government interference.
3. The main motive of the private sector is to earn profits from their business operations.

Select the correct answer using the codes given below.

(a) Only 1 (b) 1 and 2
(c) 2 and 3 (d) 1, 2 and 3

Ans. (c)

Exp. Statements (2) and (3) are correct regarding public and private sector as public and private sectors are differentiated on the basis of 'ownership of the enterprises'. In private sector, ownership of assets and delivery of services is in the hands of private individuals or companies. They are guided by the motivation to earn profits.

Statement (1) is incorrect. In case of public sector, public service and establishment of essential infrastructure are the guideing principles. In public sector, government owns the assets and is responsible for delivery of services.

14 Consider the following statements.

(Chap 2, Class-X, New NCERT)

1. Primary sector is called so because it forms the base for all other products that we subsequently make.
2. Since, most of the natural products we get are from agriculture, dairy, fishing, forestry, this sector is also called agriculture and related sectors.

Which of the statements given above is/are correct?

(a) Only 1 (b) Only 2
(c) Both 1 and 2 (d) Neither 1 nor 2

Ans. (c)

Exp. Both the statements (1) and (2) are correct.

When we produce a good by exploiting natural resources, it is an activity of primary sector. It forms the base for all other products. Since, most of the natural products we get are from agriculture, dairy, fishing and forestry, this sector is called agriculture and related sector. For example, cotton, milk production, minerals and ores.

15 **Consider the following statements.**
(Chap 2, Class-X, New NCERT)

1. Tertiary activities, by themselves, do not produce a good but they are an aid or a support for the production process.
2. Transport, banking, storage, communication and trade are some examples of tertiary activities.

Which of the statement(s) given above is/are correct?

(a) Only 1 (b) Only 2
(c) Both 1 and 2 (d) Neither 1 nor 2

Ans. (c)

Exp. Both the statements (1) and (2) are correct related to tertiary sector.
Tertiary sector helps in the development of primary and secondary sectors. These activities, by themselves do not produce a good but they are an aid and support for the production process. Since, these activities generate services rather than goods, the tertiary sector is also called the Service Sector.
For example, Transport, banking, storage, communication and trade are some examples of tertiary activities.

16 **Consider the following pairs.**
(Chap 2, Class-X, New NCERT)

	Sector	Example
1.	Quaternary	Consulting and Research and Development
2.	Quinary	Executive, official
3.	Secondary	Construction, manufacturing

How many pairs given above is/are correctly matched?

(a) Only one pair (b) Only two pairs
(c) All three pairs (d) None of the pairs

Ans. (c)

Exp. All three pairs i.e., (1), (2) and (3) are correct as Quaternary Sector is defined as the industry based on human knowledge which involved technology, information, financial planning, research and development.
The quinary sector is an important extension of the tertiary sector. The quinary sector include important organisation structures. Such as government organisations, public services, healthcare and education.
The secondary sector covers all those activities consisting in varying degree of processing of raw materials (manufacturing, construction industries).

Economic Growth & Development

17 **Consider the following statements.**
(Chap 2, Class-XI, New NCERT)

1. Usually with economic development, the share of agriculture to the GDP declines and the share of the service sector becomes dominant.
2. At higher levels of development, the industrial sector contributes more to the GDP than the service sector.

Which of the statements given above is/are correct?

(a) Only 1 (b) Only 2
(c) Both 1 and 2 (d) Neither 1 nor 2

Ans. (d)

Exp. Neither statement (1) nor (2) is correct.
The economic development of the country is usually characterised by structural changes in the economy.
At the first stage of development, the share of agriculture declines whereas share of industrial sector (not service sector) becomes dominant.
At higher levels of development, the service sector contributes more to the GDP than the other two sectors.
India is considered as exception to this traditional model of economic growth as the share of agriculture in GDP (which was 50% in early 1950s) declined and was overshadowed by the service sector, which became most important sector of the Indian economy.

18 **Consider the following statements regarding economic growth.** *(Chap 2, Class-XI, New NCERT)*

1. It refers to an increase in the country's capacity to produce the output of goods and services in an economy.
2. It implies either a larger stock of productive capital, or a larger size of supporting services like transport and banking, or an increase in the efficiency of productive capital and services.

Which of the statements given above is/are correct?

(a) Only 1 (b) Only 2
(c) Both 1 and 2 (d) Neither 1 nor 2

Ans. (c)

Exp. Both the statements (1) and (2) are correct regarding economic growth.
Economic growth is the increase in the value of an economy's goods and services. It is an increase in the capacity of an economy to produce goods and services.
A steady increase in Gross Domestic Product (GDP) is considered as good indicator of growth. It is considered as quantitative assessment of economic growth and is measured as increased stock of productive capital or services.

19 **Which of the following statements is/are correct regarding development?** *(Chap 1, Class-X, New NCERT)*

1. Different persons could have different as well as conflicting notions of a country's development.
2. Different persons can have different developmental goals.
3. Development for one, may even be destructive for the other.

Select the correct answer using the codes given below.

(a) Only 1 (b) 1 and 2 (c) 2 and 3 (d) 1, 2 and 3

Ans. (d)

Exp. All the statements (1), (2) and (3) are correct regarding development.

Different people have different developmental goals. For example, for landless labours, more days of work and better wages are the developmental goals.

On the other hand, for prosperous farmers from Punjab, high family income through higher support price for their crops will be the developmental goal.

Development for one may be destructive for others.

For example, for better supply of electricity, an industrialist may want to construct more dams but construction of dams lead to displacement of lot of people.

20 Consider the following pairs. *(Chap 1, Class-X, New NCERT)*

	Country	Plan/Years
1.	India	Programme (1958)
2.	China	First-Five Year Plan (1951)
3.	Pakistan	First-Five Year Plan (1956)

How many pairs given above is/are correctly matched?

(a) Only one pair (b) Only two pairs
(c) All three pairs (d) None of the pairs

Ans. (a)

Exp. Only one pair i.e., (3) is correctly matched as Pakistan announced its First-Five Year Plan called the Medium Term Development Plan in 1956.

However, pairs (1) and (2) are not correctly matched.

The Great leap forward programme was a five-year economic plan executed by Mao Zedong and the Chinese Communist Party begun in 1958 and abandoned in 1961.

The First-Five Year Plan was launched in 1951 in India, which mainly focused in the development of the primary sector.

21 Which of the following are considered to be the four pillars of human development? *(Chap 3, Class-XII, New NCERT)*

(a) Equity, inclusion, productivity and empowerment.
(b) Equity, productivity, empowerment and sustainability.
(c) Productivity, gender, inclusion and equity.
(d) Labour, productivity, inclusion and equity.

Ans. (b)

Exp. Equity, productivity, empowerment and sustainability are considered to be the four pillars of human development.

Equity refers to making equal access to opportunities available to everybody.

Productivity means enrichment of human capital and empowerment refers to power to make choices. Sustainability means continuity in the availability of opportunities.

22 Which of the following statements is incorrect regarding the difference between physical capital and human capital? *(Chap 5, Class-XI, New NCERT)*

(a) Physical capital is intangible and human capital is tangible.
(b) Physical capital can be easily sold in the market whereas human capital is not sold in the market.
(c) The physical capital is separable from its owner, whereas, human capital is inseparable from its owner.
(d) None of the above

Ans. (a)

Exp. Statement (a) is incorrect regarding the difference between physical capital and human capital as physical capital is tangible and can be easily sold in the market like any other commodity on the other hand, human capital is intangible and is not sold in the market. Only the services of the human capital are sold.

23 With reference to Human development, which of the following statement is/are correct? *(Chap 4, Class-XI, New NCERT)*

1. It is a process that enlarges people's choices and improve their lives.
2. Equity, sustainability, productivity and empowerment are the four pillars of Human development.
3. Development means a qualitative change which is always value positive.
4. The concept of Human development was introduced by Dr. Mahbub-ul-Haq.

How many of the statements given above is/are correct?

(a) Only one (b) Only two (c) Only three (d) All four

Ans. (d)

Exp. All four statements are correct with reference to Human development. It is defined as the process of enlarging people's freedoms and opportunities and improving their well-being. Equity, sustainability, productivity and empowerment are the four pillars of Human development.

Development means a qualitative change like growth of intelligence, creativity, morality and its value always positive. It was developed by economist Dr. Mahbub-ul-Haq.

24 With reference to the Human Development Report, 2021-22, which of the following statements is/are correct? *(Chap 1, Class-X, New NCERT), (UPPCS Pre 2023)*

1. India's rank on the Human Development Index has upgraded from 130 in 2020 to 132 in 2022.
2. India's rank on the Human Development Index has stipped from 130 in 2020 to 132 in 2022.

Select the correct answer using the code given below.

(a) Only 1 (b) Only 2
(c) Both 1 and 2 (d) Neither 1 nor 2

Ans. (d)

Exp. Neither statement (1) nor (2) is correct with respect to Human Development Report 2021-22. In the 2020 report, India had ranked 131st among 189 countries. The decline in the country's performance from its level was on account of a fall in its life expectancy. India's HDI is ranked 132 out of 191 countries in 2022 Human Development report while India's rank on the HDI in 2020 was 131.

25 **Consider the following statements.**

(Chap 5, Class-XI, New NCERT)

1. Physical capital is completely mobile between countries except for some artificial trade restrictions.
2. Human capital is not perfectly mobile between countries as movement is restricted by nationality and culture.

Which of the statements given above is/are correct?

(a) Only 1 (b) Only 2
(c) Both 1 and 2 (d) Neither 1 nor 2

Ans. (c)

Exp. Both the statements (1) and (2) are correct. Physical capital does not require presence of owner, it is tangible and it is completely mobile. Its formation can be built even through imports whereas human capital is not perfectly mobile between countries as movement is restricted by nationality and culture. Its formation is to be done through conscious policy formulations in consonance with the nature of the society and economy and expenditure by the state and the individuals.

26 **Which of the following statements is/are correct about human development in Indian context?**

(Chap 2, Class-IX, New NCERT)

(a) The expenditure on education has constantly increased over the last 5 years.
(b) The expenditure on health has constantly decreased over the last 5 years.
(c) Literacy among males is nearly 14.4% higher than females and it is about 16% higher in urban areas as compared to rural areas.
(d) All of the above

Ans. (c)

Exp. Statement (c) is correct about human development. As per Census 2011, the literacy rate at all India level is 72.98% and the literacy rate for females and males are 64.63% and 80.9% respectively. Thus, literacy among males is nearly 14.4% higher than females. In the rural areas, the literacy rate is 68.91% and in urban, it is 84.98%, hence, literacy rate is about 16% higher in urban areas as compared to rural areas.

27 **Consider the following statements.**

(Chap 4, Class-XI, New NCERT)

1. The Multi-dimensional Poverty Index was launched by the United Nations Development Programme (UNDP) and the Oxford Poverty and Human Development Initiative in 2010.
2. It is based on the idea that poverty is not unidimensional.
3. It uses three dimensions and ten indicators.

How many of the statement given above is/are correct?

(a) Only one (b) Only two (c) All three (d) None of these

Ans. (c)

Exp. All three statements i.e., (1), (2) and (3) are correct. Mult-idimensional Poverty was developed in 2010 by the Oxford Poverty and Human Development initiative and the United Nations Development Programme. It is based on the idea that poverty is not unidimensional.
The index shows the proportion of poor people and the average number of deprivation each poor person experiences at the same time. MPI uses three dimensions, health, education and standard of livings and ten indicators to determine the intensity of poverty.

28 **Consider the following Assertion(A) and Reason (R) and choose the correct code.**

(Chap 5, Class-XI, New NCERT)

Assertion (A) Human development is based on the idea that education and health are integral to human well-being.
Reason (R) Only when people have the ability to read and write and the ability to lead a long and healthy life, they will be able to make other choices, which they value.

Codes

(a) Both A and R are true and R is the correct explanation of A.
(b) Both A and R are true, but R is incorrect explanation of A.
(c) A is true, but R is false.
(d) A is false, but R is true.

Ans. (a)

Exp. Both Assertion (A) and Reason (R) are true and Reason (R) is the correct explanation of Assertion (A). Human development is based on the idea that education and health are integral to human well-being. It is because only possible when the people have the ability to read and write alongwith the ability to lead a long and healthy life, then they will be able to make other choices which they value. There for every individual has the right to get basic education and basic healthcare i.e., every individual has the right to be literate and lead a healthy life.

29 **Which of the following is the meaning of people as a resource?** *(Chap 5, Class-XI, New NCERT)*

(a) It means people are the natural capital of a country based no their existing skills.
(b) It means that people are the human capital of a country based on their existing skills.
(c) It means that people are the technical capital to a country based on their existing skills.
(d) It means that people are the overall capital of a country based on their existing skills.

Ans. (b)

Exp. Statement (b) is correct meaning of people as a resource. 'People as a resource' refers to a country's working people in terms of their existing productive skills and abilities.

The population becomes human capital when an investment is made in the form of education and training.

30 Consider the following statements.

(Chap 9, Class-XI, New NCERT)

1. India supports approximately 17% of the world's human and 20% of livestock population on a mere 2.5% of the world's geographical area.
2. The CPCB (Central Pollution Control Board) has identified seventeen categories of industries (large and medium scale) as significantly polluting.

Which of the statements given above is/are correct?

(a) Only 1
(b) Only 2
(c) Both 1 and 2
(d) Neither 1 nor 2

Ans. (c)

Exp. Both the statements (1) and (2) are correct.

India supports approximately 17% of the world's human and 20% of livestock population on a mere 2.5% of the world's geographical area. The high density of population and livestock and the competing use of land for forestry, agriculture, etc. exert enormous pressure on the country's resources.

The CPCB (Central Pollution Control Board) has identified seventeen categories of industries (large and medium scale) as significantly polluting.

31 Consider the following Assertion(A) and Reason (R) and choose the correct code.

(Chap 9, Class-XI, New NCERT)

Assertion (A) Development that ignores its repercussions on the environment will destroy the environment that sustains life forms.

Reason (R) Environment and economy are interdependent and need each other.

Codes

(a) Both A and R are true and R is the correct explanation of A.
(b) Both A and R are true, but R is incorrect explanation of A.
(c) A is true, but R is false.
(d) A is false, but R is true.

Ans. (a)

Exp. Both Assertion (A) and Reason (R) are true and Reason (R) is the correct explanation of Assertion (A).

Development that ignores its repercussions on the environment will destroy the environment that sustains life forms.

Environment and economy are interdependent and need each other. For that, they need sustainable development, which is a development that will allow all future generations to have a potential average quality of life.

32 Which of the following statements is/are correct regarding Sustainable Development?

(Chap 9, Class-XI, New NCERT),

1. It ensures the well being of individuals by integrating social development, economic development, environmental conservation and protection.
2. It was set up in 2015 by the United Nations General Assembly and are intended to be achieved by the year 2030.
3. It is a collection of 17 interlinked global goals for a better future for all.

Select the correct answer using the codes given below.

(a) Only 1
(b) 1 and 2
(c) 2 and 3
(d) 1, 2 and 3

Ans. (d)

Exp. All the statements are correct with reference to Sustainable Development.

It ensures the well being of individuals by integrating social economic development and environment conservation. It is a broad term to describe policies, projects and investments that provide benefits today without sacrificing environmental, social and personal health in the future.

The Sustainable Development Goals (SDGs) were adopted by the United Nations General Assembly in 2015 as a universal call to action to end poverty, protect the planet, and ensure that by 2030 all people enjoy peace and prosperity. The SDGs are a collection of 17 goals that are designed to end poverty, hunger, AIDS, and discrimination against women and girls.

33 Match List-I with List-II and select the correct answer using the codes given below the lists.

(Chap 4, Class-XI, New NCERT)

List-I (Substainable Development Goal)	List-II (Related With)
A. SDG-10	1. Climate action
B. SDG-13	2. Life on land
C. SDG-14	3. Reduction inequalities
D. SDG-15	4. Life below water

Codes

	A	B	C	D
(a)	2	3	1	4
(b)	3	1	4	2
(c)	3	2	4	1
(d)	1	2	3	4

Ans. (b)

Exp. The correct matching is A-3, B-1, C-4, D-2.

SDG-10 is about reduction in inequalities within and among countries.

SDG-13 Calls to take urgent action to combat climate change and its impact.

SDG-14 is about conserving and sustainably using the oceans, seas and marine resources.

SDG-15 aims to protect, restore and promote sustainable use of terrestrial ecosystem.

Chapter 02

National Income and Accounting

National Income and Accounting

National Income

Introduction
- Complete value of total goods and services known as NI
- First attempt to calculate NI in 1868 by **Dadabhai Naoroji**
- The Government of India appointed a National Income Committee under the chairmanship of **Dr. PC Mahalanobis**
- This committee gave its first report in 1951 and final report in 1954
- Committee estimated National Income of ₹ 8650 crore and Per Capita Income of ₹ 246.50

Basic terms used in NI and Accounting
- **Final Goods** Such goods that are meant for final use
- **Intermediate Goods** Such goods are used by other producers as material inputs
- **Depreciation** It is an annual allowance for wear and tear of capital goods
- **Market Price** It refers to the actual transacted price and it includes indirect taxes
- **Factor Cost** It includes government grants and subsidies, but it excludes indirect taxes
- **Purchasing Power Parity** The PPP exchange rates are constructed to ensure that the same quantity of goods and services are priced equivalently across countries
- **Base Year** It is the year against which the performance of an index is measured
- **Hindu Growth Rate** The Hindu rate of growth is a term referring to the low annual growth rate of the planned economy of India before the liberalisation of 1991

Various Measures of National Income
- Gross Domestic Product (GDP)
- Monetary value of all finished goods and services during a specified period
- GDP = C + I + G

Gross Value Added (GVA)
- Measure the contribution of growth made by individual sector
- GVA = GDP + Subsidies on products – Taxes on products

Gross National Product (GNP)
- Count all the output of the resident/ national of a country
- GNP=GDP + X – I

Net Domestic Product
- Difference between Gross & Net Domestic Product
- NDP=GDP- Depreciation

Net National Product (NNP)
- Deduct Depreciation from GNP
- NNP–GNP–Depreciation

Per Capita Income (PCI)
- Measure the average income earned per person
- $PCI - \frac{\text{National Income}}{\text{Total Population}}$

Green Gross Domestic Product (GGDP)
- Index of economic growth with environmental consequences
- Monetises the loss of biodiversity and accounts for costs caused by climate change

Calculation of National Income

NI=C+I+G(X-M)

Formula of Calculating National Income

NI = C + I + G (X-M)

C = Consumption expenditure
I = Investment
X = Total exports
M = Total imports
G = Government expenditure

Various Methods of Measuring National Income

Product Method
- Also known as output method or value added method
- Calculate the aggregate value of final goods and service in a year
- It breaks down production process into various stage to calculate GDP, value added is summed up at each stage of production

Income Method
- Sum of net income earned by working people in different sectors

NI = (Total rent – Income from land) + (Total Wages – Income from Labour) + (Total Interest – Income from Capital) + (Total Profit – Income from Entrepreneur)

Consumption Method
- Combination of production method and income method
- NI = Total Consumption Expenditure + Total Savings

SOURCE **New NCERT Class X** (Sectors of the Indian Economy), **New NCERT Class X** (Development), **New NCERT Class XI** (Indian Economy on the Eve of Independence), **Old NCERT Class XI** (Composition of Macroeconomy and Accounting of Natural Income), **New NCERT Class XII** (Accounting of National Income), **Old NCERT Class XII** (Accounting of National Income : Concepts and Measurement), **Tamil Nadu Board Class XII** (National Income)

1 **Consider the following statements.**

(Chap 3, Class-XI, Old NCERT)

1. Dadabhai Naoroji made the first crude estimates of National income in 1868 in his book 'Poverty and Un-British Rule in India'.
2. In 1934 VKRV Rao published 'An Essay on India's National Income' 1925-29, which is regarded as the first authentic estimation of the National income of India.
3. The Government of India appointed the 'National Income Committee' in 1949 under the chairmanship of prof PC Mahalanobis.

How many of the statements given above is/are correct?

(a) Only one (b) Only two (c) All three (d) None of these

Ans. (c)

Exp. All three statements i.e., (1), (2) and (3) are correct as the first attempt to calculate National income of India was made by Dadabhai Naoroji who estimated National income by first estimating the value of agricultural production and then adding a certain percentage as non-agricultural production. This was however a non-scientific method. The first person to adopt a scientific procedure in estimating national income was Dr. VKRV Rao in 1925-29. He divided the Indian economy into two parts

(i) Agricultural sector which included agriculture, forests, fishing and hunting.
(ii) Corporate sector which included industries, construction, business, transport and public services.

The first official attempt was made by Prof. PC Mahalanobis in 1951. The committee estimated national income of ₹ 8650 crore and per capital income of ₹ 246.50.

2 **Consider the following statements regarding types of goods.** *(Chap 3, Class-XII, New NCERT)*

1. Goods like food and clothing and services like recreation that are consumed when purchased by their ultimate consumers are called Capital goods.
2. Goods that are meant for final use and will not pass through any more stages of production is called Final goods.

Which of the statements given above is/are correct?

(a) Only 1 (b) Only 2
(c) Both 1 and 2 (d) Neither 1 nor 2

Ans. (b)

Exp. Only statement (2) is correct regarding to the types of goods. Consumer goods also called Final goods are the finished products that consumers buy after the production process. It is the end result of production and manufacturing. Clothing, food products and dishwashers are examples of common consumer goods.

While statement (1) is incorrect as capital goods are the tangible assets used to produce products to create finished products. Capital goods are not commonly sold to consumers but are used to produce other goods, which are sold to consumers.

3 **The national income of a country for a given period is equal to the** *(Chap 2, Class-XII, New NCERT)* ***(IAS Pre 2013)***

(a) total value of goods and services produced by the nationals
(b) sum of total consumption and investment expenditure
(c) sum of personal income of all individuals
(d) money value of final goods and services produced

Ans. (d)

Exp. The national income of a country for a given period is equal to the money value of final goods and services produced. In India, it is calculated by using combined method consisting of product/output and income method.

4 **Consider the following statements.**

(Chap 2, Class-XII, New NCERT)

1. National income is the monetary value of all final goods and services produced in India.
2. Depreciation is deducted from gross value to get the net value.

Which of the statements given above is/are correct?

(a) Only 1 (b) Only 2
(c) Both 1 and 2 (d) Neither 1 nor 2

Ans. (c)

Exp. Both the statements (1) and (2) given above are correct as National income is the sum total of the value of all the goods and services manufactured by the residents of the country, in a year within its domestic boundaries or outside. It is the net amount of income of the citizens by production in a year.

Depreciation is the measure of the decreased monetary value of and asset over time due to use, wear and tear. It is deducted from gross value to get the net value.

NNP (Net National Product) = GNP (Gross National Product) – Depreciation

5 **Among the following which countries are above India in terms of nominal GDP as per data of IMF (year 2020)?** *(Chap 2, Class-XII, Tamil Nadu Board)* ***(Tripura PCS Pre 2023)***

(a) US, China, Japan, Germany (b) China, UK, US, Germany
(c) US, China, UK, Japan (d) China, US, France, UK

Ans. (a)

Exp. US, China, Japan and Germany are above India in terms of nominal GDP as per data of International Monetary Fund (IMF). Countries are sorted by nominal GDP estimates from financial and statistical institutions, which are calculated at market or government official exchange rates. Nominal GDP does not take into account differences in the cost of living in different countries. Comparisons of national wealth are also frequently made on the basis of Purchasing Power Parity (PPP), to adjust for differences in the cost of living in different countries. Other metrics, nominal GDP per capita and a corresponding GDP (PPP) per capita are used for comparing national standard of living.

6 **Consider the following pairs.** *(Chap 2, Class-X, New NCERT)*

1. Final Goods – does not undergo any further transformation.
2. Intermediate Goods – raw material or inputs for production of other commodities.
3. Consumer Goods – food and clothing, and services like recreation.

How many pairs given above is/are incorrectly matched?

(a) Only one
(b) Only two
(c) Only three
(d) None of the above

Ans. (d)

Exp. None of the given pairs is incorrectly matched.

Final goods is such an item that is meant for final use and will not pass through any more stages of production or transformation start with first term. These items are ready to be sold finally to the consumers for final use. e.g., readymade garments.

Intermediate goods are those that don't end up in final consumption and are not capital goods either. They are mostly used as raw materials or inputs for production of other commodities.

For example, steel sheet is an intermediate good used for making automobile.

Consumer goods are those goods like food and clothing and services like recreation that are consumed when purchased by their ultimate consumers.

7 **Consider the following statements.** *(Chap 2, Class-XII, New NCERT)*

1. Depreciation is an annual allowance for damage of capital goods.
2. Depreciation does not take into account unexpected or sudden destruction of capital by accident, natural calamities or other such extraneous circumstances.

Which of the statements given above is/are correct?

(a) Only 1
(b) Only 2
(c) Both 1 and 2
(d) Neither 1 nor 2

Ans. (c)

Exp. Both the statements (1) and (2) are correct.

Depreciation is reduction in value of an asset over a period of time.

For example, a machine of pen making cost is ₹ 10 lakh. After five years of use, the cost value of the machine will reduce due to its continuous use.

Depreciation does not take into account unexpected or sudden destruction or disuse of capital by an accident, natural calamities or other extraneous circumstances.

8 **Match the following lists correctly and choose the correct code.** *(Chap 2, Class-XII, New NCERT)*

List-I (Factors)	List-II (Facts)
A. GDP_{MP}	1. Income earned by the factors in the form of wages, profits, rents, interest etc, within the domestic territory of country.
B. NDP_{FC}	2. Accounting tool developed by United Nation to measure national income.
C. SNA 2008	3. Consumption of fixed capital.
D. Depreciation	4. Market value of all final goods and services produced within a domestic territory of a country measured in a year.

Codes

	A	B	C	D		A	B	C	D
(a)	2	1	3	4	(b)	4	1	2	3
(c)	3	1	4	2	(d)	1	2	3	4

Ans. (b)

Exp. The correct matching is A-4, B-1, C-2, D-3.

Gross Domestic Product at Market Prices (GDP_{MP}) It is the market value of all final goods and services produced within a domestic territory of a country measured in a year. It is calculated as $GDP_{MP} = C + I + G + X - M$, Where C = private consumption, I = investment, G = purchase and X – M = foreign expenditure.

Net Domestic Product at Factor Cost (NDP_{FC}) It is the income earned in the form of wages, profits, rents, interest etc, within the domestic territory of a country. It is calculated as NDP_{FC} = NDP (market price) - Net Product Taxes - Net Production Taxes.

System of National Accounts, 2008 (SNA 2008). It is an accounting tool developed by United Nations to measure national income. India shifted to this methodology in 2015.

Depreciation It is also known as consumption of fixed capital. It is an annual allowance for wear and tear of a capital goods.

9 **After 2015, which of the following calculation by National Statistical Office (NSO) represents the National income?** *(Chap 2, Class-XII, New NCERT)*

1. GDP at Market Price
2. GVA at Basic Price
3. GDP at Factor Cost

Codes

(a) 1 and 3
(b) 1 and 2
(c) 1, 2 and 3
(d) None of these

Ans. (b)

Exp. Options (1) and (2) are correct as after 2015, the National Statistical Office (NSO) replaced GDP at factor cost with the GVA at basic prices, and the GDP at market prices, which is now called only GDP.

Gross Value Added (GVA) is the value of total output produced in the economy less the value of intermediate consumption. The basic price includes the production taxes but not product taxes.

Thus, GVA at basic prices = GVA at market price − Net product taxes.

GDP at market price is the market value of all final goods and services produced within a domestic territory of a country measured in a year.

Thus, GDP_{MP} = Total production + Taxes − Subsidies.

Statement (3) is incorrect as GDP at factor cost is the total value of goods and commodities produced in a year in a country by its all production units. GDP at factor cost is not taken in calculation by NSO.

10 Consider the following statements.

Statement-I Gross National Product (GDP) is GDP plus net factor income from abroad.

Statement-II Net Domestic Product at factor cost is also known as National income.

(Chap 2, Class-XII, New NCERT)

Which one of the following is correct in respect of the above statements?

(a) Both Statement-I and Statement-II are correct and Statement-II is the correct explanation for Statement-I.

(b) Both Statement-I and Statement-II are correct and Statement-II is not the correct explanation for Statement-I.

(c) Statement-I is correct but Statement-II is incorrect.

(d) Statement-I is incorrect but Statement-II is correct.

Ans. (c)

Exp. Statement-I is correct but Statement-II is incorrect.

Statement I is correct as Gross National Product (GNP) is Gross Domestic Product (GDP) plus net factor income from abroad. It measures the monetary value of all the finished goods and services produced by the country's factors of production irrespective of their location. Therefore, GNP = GDP + factor income earned by the domestic factors of production employed in the rest of the world − factor income earned by the factors of production of the rest of the world in the domestic economy.

Statement-II is incorrect as Domestic factor income is another name for NDP (at factor cost). NDP(at factor cost) stands for Net Domestic Product or Domestic Income.

Formula NDP (at factor cost) = GDP (at market price) − Depreciation − Net Indirect tax.

Net National Product at Factor Cost (NNP_{FC}) is known as National Income.

11 Which of the following statements is/are incorrect about Net National Product (NNP)?

(Chap 2, Class-XII, New NCERT)

1. It shows net production of goods and services produced in a given financial year adjusted for net factor income from abroad.
2. It includes exports, imports, but not factor income from abroad.
3. It is called 'net' because it deducts capital depreciation from total National income.

Select the correct answer using the codes given below.

(a) Only 1 (b) Only 2
(c) Both 1 and 2 (d) Neither 1 nor 2

Ans. (b)

Exp. Only statement (2) is incorrect about Net National Product (NNP). Net National Product (NNP) is the monetary value of finished goods and services produced by a country's citizens, overseas and domestically, in a given period. It is the equivalent of Gross National Product (GNP), the total value of a nation's annual output, minus the amount of GNP required to purchase new goods to maintain existing stock, otherwise known as Depreciation.

Net National Product (NNP) = Gross National Product (GNP) − Depreciation

12 Consider the following statements.

(Chap 2, Class-XII, Old NCERT)

1. GVA (Gross Value Added) is the measure of the value of goods and services produced in an area.
2. GVA adjusts Gross Domestic Product (GDP) by the impact of subsidies and taxes on product.

Which of the statements given above is/are correct?

(a) Only 1 (b) Only 2
(c) Both 1 and 2 (d) Neither 1 nor 2

Ans. (c)

Exp. Both the statements (1) and (2) are correct about GVA (Gross Value Added).

Gross Value Added (GVA) is an economic productivity that measures the contribution of a corporate subsidiary, company or municipality to an economy, producer, sector or region.

GVA is the output of the country minus the intermediate consumption (at purchaser price) which is the difference between gross output and net output.

GVA is important because it is used to adjust GDP, which is a key indicator of the state of a nation's total economy.

13 Which of the following is/are not included in the calculation of National income?

(Chap 3, Class-XII, Old NCERT)

1. transfer payment by the government
2. private transfers
3. production for self-consumption

Codes

(a) 1 and 3 (b) 1 and 2 (c) 2 and 3 (d) All of these

Ans. (d)

Exp. All the given factors are not included in the calculation of National income.

National Income or Net National Product at factor cost = NNP at market prices − (Indirect taxes − subsidies)

Thus, transfer payment by the government, private transfers and production for self-consumption are not included in national income.

14 With reference to estimation of National income, which of the following statements is/are correct? *(Chap 2, Class-XII, New NCERT)*

1. Land, Labour, Capital and Entrepreneurship are considered as four factors of production.
2. Spending on intermediate goods are included as final expenditure for estimation of National income.

Codes

(a) Only 1 (b) Only 2
(c) Both 1 and 2 (d) Neither 1 nor 2

***Ans.* (a)**

Exp. Only statement (1) is correct with reference to estimation of National income as Land, Labour Capital and Entrepreneurship are considered as four factors of production. These factors include, rents, wages, interest and profits respectively. It is used to calculate National income.

Statement (2) is incorrect as spending on intermediate goods are not included as final expenditure for estimation of national income to avoid the problem of double counting. These goods are used for manufacturing of final products. For examples, tyres are used for the manufacturing of final product in cars.

15 Consider the following statements. *(Chap 2, Class-XII, New NCERT)*

1. Market price includes indirect taxes and government subsidies.
2. Factor cost includes government grants and subsidies.
3. Base year is also called the Reference Year.

Which of the statements given above is/are correct?

(a) Only 3 (b) 1 and 2 (c) 2 and 3 (d) All of these

***Ans.* (d)**

Exp. All the given statements (1), (2) and (3) are correct.

Market price refers to the actual transacted price and it includes indirect taxes (excise duty, VAT, service tax etc.) and government subsidies.

The factor cost means the total cost of all factors of production consumed or used in producing a good or service. It includes government grants and subsidies, but it excludes indirect taxes. The year against which the performance of an index is measured is called Base Year. It is also called the Reference Year.

16 A decrease in tax to GDP ratio of a country indicates which of the following? *(Chap 3, Class-XII, New NCERT)*

1. Slowing economic growth rate
2. Less equitable distribution of national income

Select the correct answer using the codes given below.

(a) Only 1
(b) Only 2
(c) Both 1 and 2
(d) Neither 1 nor 2

***Ans.* (a)**

Exp. Only statement (1) is correct as the tax-to-GDP ratio is a ratio of a nation's tax revenue relative to its Gross Domestic Product (GDP).

The Tax-to-GDP ratio is used to compare tax receipts from year to year. As taxes are related to economic activity, the ratio should stay relatively consistent. When the gross domestic product (GDP) grows, tax revenue should increase as well.

Economic slowdown results in lower rates of growth, where unemployment usually rises and consumer spending decreases. As a result, the Tax-to-GDP ratio declines.

Statement (2) is incorrect as the less equitable distribution of national income is not directly related to decrease in tax to GDP ratio. Equal distribution of national income and resource allocation generally depends upon the economic planning of a country.

17 With reference to Indian economy, consider the following statements. *(Chap 2, Class-XII, New NCERT)*

1. The rate of growth of Real Gross Domestic Product has steadily increased in the last decade.
2. The Gross Domestic Product at market price (in rupees) has steadily increased in the last decade.

Which of the statements given above is/are correct?

(a) Only 1 (b) Only 2
(c) Both 1 and 2 (d) Neither 1 nor 2

***Ans.* (b)**

Exp. Only statement (2) is correct as the GDP at market prices of India has steadily increased in the last decade from around 900 billion USD in 2005 to 2.1 trillion USD in 2015. As of 2023 India's GDP is 3.73 trillion USD.

Statement (1) is incorrect as the rate of growth of real GDP has not steadily increased in the last decade. It has fluctuated due to various international and domestic economic pressures.

Gross Domestic Product (GDP) is the monetary value of all the final goods and services produced within a country's borders in a specific time period, generally one year. It is a broad measurement of a nation's overall economic activity.

Real Gross Domestic Product is an inflation-adjusted measure that reflects the value of all goods and services produced by an economy in a given year, expressed in base-year prices.

18 Consider the following statements. *(Chap 2, Class-XII, New NCERT)*

1. The profit earned by Korean-owned Hyundai car factory is included in GNP of India.
2. The change in the inventory of a firm is treated as investment.
3. GDP deflator is considered as the best tool to measure change of prices in an economy as it includes all goods and services.

(a) 1 and 2 (b) 2 and 3
(c) 1 and 3 (d) All of these

Ans. (b)

Exp. Statements (2) and (3) are correct. The unsold stock of goods and materials is known as Inventory and Treated as Capital. Addition to the stock of capital of a firm is known as Investment. Therefore, change in the inventory of a firm is treated as investment.

The reason why GDP deflator (Implicit Price Deflator) is considered as the best tool to measure change of prices in an economy as it includes all goods and services.

Statement (1) is incorrect as Gross National Product (GNP) measures the total value of all finished goods and services produced by a country's citizen in a given financial year, irrespective of their location. Therefore, profit earned by Korean-owned Hyundai car factory is included in Korean GNP.

19 Consider the following statements. *(Chap 2, Class-XII, New NCERT)*

1. Nominal GDP is calculated in a way such that, the goods and services are evaluated at some constant set of prices.
2. Real GDP, on the other hand, is simply the value of GDP at the current prevailing prices.

Which of the statements given above is/are correct?

(a) Only 1 (b) Only 2
(c) Both 1 and 2 (d) Neither 1 nor 2

Ans. (d)

Exp. Neither statement (1) nor (2) is correct.

Nominal GDP is the value of GDP at the current prevailing prices, on the other hand, real GDP is calculated in a way such that goods and services are evaluated at some constant set of prices or constant prices. Since, these prices remain fixed, if the real GDP changes, we can be sure that it is the volume of production which is undergoing the changes.

The ratio of nominal GDP to real GDP gives us an idea of how the prices have moved from the base year to the current year.

20 Consider the following statements. *(Chap 2, Class-XII, New NCERT)*

1. If the GDP of the country is rising, welfare always arises as a consequence.
2. If we relate welfare improvement in the country to the percentage of people who are better off, then GDP is not a good index.

Which of the statements given above is/are incorrect?

(a) Only 1 (b) Only 2
(c) Both 1 and 2 (d) Neither 1 nor 2

Ans. (a)

Exp. Only statement (1) is incorrect because if the GDP of the country is rising, the welfare may not rise as a consequence.

This is because the rise in GDP may be concentrated in the hands of very few individuals or firms. For the rest, the income may infact have fallen.

In such a case, the welfare of the entire country cannot be said to have increased.

21 Consider the following statements. *(Chap 2, Class-XII, New NCERT)*

1. The year whose prices are being used to calculate the real GDP is known as the Base Year.
2. The prices calculated at base year is known as Basic Price.

Which of the statements given above is/are correct?

(a) Only 1 (b) Only 2
(c) Both 1 and 2 (d) Neither 1 nor 2

Ans. (c)

Exp. Both the statements (1) and (2) are correct.

The year whose prices are being used to calculate the real GDP is known as the 'Base Year'. As of October, 2021, the base year for GDP in India is 2011-12.

The prices calculated at base year is known as Basic Price.

22 Match the following lists correctly and choose the correct code. *(Chap 2, Class-XII, New NCERT)*

List-I (Income Determinant)	List-II (Description)
A. Marginal propensity to consume	1. Change in consumption per unit change in income
B. Marginal propensity to save	2. Change in savings per unit change in income
C. Average propensity to consume	3. Consumption expenditures per unit of disposable income
D. Average propensity to save	4. Savings per unit of income

Codes

	A	B	C	D
(a)	1	2	3	4
(b)	4	3	2	1
(c)	1	3	2	4
(d)	1	2	4	3

Ans. (a)

Exp. The correct matching is A-1, B-2, C-3, D-4.

Marginal propensity to consume It is the change in consumption per unit change in income. In other words, it is the proportion of an aggregate raise in pay that a consumer spends on the consumption of goods and services, as opposed to saving it.

Marginal propensity to save It is the change in saving per unit change in income. In other words, it is the fraction of an increase in income that is not spent and instead used for saving.

Average propensity to consume It is the consumption expenditures per unit of disposable income.

Average propensity to save It is the saving per unit of income. It is usually expressed as a percentage of total household disposable income.

23 Consider the following statements.
(Chap 2, Class-XII, New NCERT)

1. Externalities refer to the benefits or harms a firm or an individual causes to another for which they are not paid or penalised.
2. Externalities do not have any market in which they can be bought and sold.

Which of the statement(s) given above is/are correct?
(a) Only 1 (b) Only 2
(c) Both 1 and 2 (d) Neither 1 nor 2

Ans. (c)

Exp. Both the statements (1) and (2) are correct.
Externalities refer to the benefits or harms a firm or an individual causes to another for which they are not paid. Externalities do not have any market in which they can be bought and sold.
For example, there is oil refinery which refines crude oil and sells it in the market. The output of refinery is the amount of oil it refines. The value added of the refinery will be counted as part of GDP.

24 Consider the following statements regarding per capita income. *(Chap 2, Class-XII, Tamil Nadu Board)*

1. Per capita income is a measure of the amount of money earned per person in a nation or region.
2. It is calculated by dividing the country's national income by its population.
3. It can be used to determine the average per-person income for an area.

Which of the above statements is/are correct?
(a) Only 1 (b) 2 and 3 (c) 1 and 3 (d) 1, 2 and 3

Ans. (d)

Exp. Statements (1), (2) and (3) are correct regarding per capita income as per capita income is a measure of the amount of money earned per person in a nation or geographic region.
It is used to determine the average per-person income for an area and to evaluate the standard of living and quality of life of the population. Per capita income for a nation is calculated by dividing the country's national income by its population.

25 Consider the following statements.
(Class-XI, Old NCERT)

1. Net Domestic Product = Gross Domestic Product – Depreciation
2. Per Capita Income = Net Domestic Product/ Total Population of the Nation

Which of the statements given above is/are correct?
(a) Only 1 (b) Only 2
(c) Both 1 and 2 (d) Neither 1 nor 2

Ans. (c)

Exp. Both statements (1) and (2) are correct as Net Domestic Product (NDP) is an annual measure of the economic output of a nation that is adjusted to account for depreciation.
It is calculated by subtracting depreciation from the Gross Domestic Product (GDP).
An increase in NDP would indicate growing economic health, while a decrease would indicate economic slowdown.
Per capital income for a nation is calculated by dividing the country's national income by its population.

26 Consider the following statements.
(Class-XI, Old NCERT)

1. Real GDP is calculated in a way such that the goods and services are evaluated at constant prices.
2. Nominal GDP is the value of GDP at the current prevailing prices.
3. The ratio of real GDP to Nominal is known as Index of Prices (GDP Deflator)

Which of the statements given above is/are correct?
(a) 1 and 2 (b) 2 and 3
(c) 1, 2 and 3 (d) 1 and 3

Ans. (a)

Exp. Statements (1) and (2) are correct as Real Gross Domestic Product is an inflation-adjusted measure that reflects the value of all goods and services produced by an economy in a given year. It is expressed in base-year prices and is referred to as Constant-price.
Real GDP makes comparing GDP more meaningful because it shows comparisons for both the quantity and value of goods and services. Real GDP is calculated by dividing nominal GDP by a GDP deflator. Unlike real GDP, nominal GDP uses current market prices and doesn't factor inflation into its calculation.
Statement (3) is incorrect as the ratio of nominal to real GDP is known as Index of Prices. This is called GDP deflator.

$$\text{GDP deflator} = \frac{\text{Nominal GDP}}{\text{Real GDP}} \times 100$$

27 Consider the following statements.
(Chap 2, Class-XII, New NCERT)

1. Green GDP is defined as data obtained after the deduction of the cost of resources, environment and human health from the tradition GDP.
2. In 2006, the Japanese Government released its Green GDP for Yangshan Deep-Water Port.

Which of the statements given above is/are correct?
(a) Only 1 (b) Only 2
(c) Both 1 and 2 (d) Neither 1 nor 2

Ans. (a)

Exp. Only statement (1) is correct.
Green GDP is defined as data obtained after the deduction of the costs of resources, environment and human health from the traditional GDP.
The 'Green GDP' is derived from Net Domestic Product (NDP), which is obtained by subtracting the depreciation of produced assets such as machines and buildings from

GDP - by deducting the cost of depletion of natural resources and degradation of ecosystems.

Statement (2) is incorrect. In 2006, the Chinese Government released its Green GDP for Yangshan Deep Water Port .

28 Consider the following statements.

(Chap 2, Class-XII, New NCERT)

1. Gross Value Added (GVA) will include production taxes and exclude production subsidies.
2. GVA at factor cost included no taxes and excluded no subsidies.

Which of the statements given above is/are correct?

(a) Only 1
(b) Only 2
(c) Both 1 and 2
(d) Neither 1 nor 2

Ans. (c)

Exp. Both statements (1) and (2) are correct as GVA at basic prices will include production taxes and excludes production subsidies available on the commodity. On the other, GVA at factor cost includes no taxes and excludes no subsidies and GDP at market prices include both production and product taxes and excludes both production and product subsidies.

The relationship between GVA at factor cost and GVA at Basic prices and GDP at market prices and GVA at Basic prices is shown below.

GVA at factor cost + (Production taxes less Production Subsidies) = GVA at basic prices.

GDP at market prices = GVA at basic prices + Product taxes – Product subsidies.

29 Consider the following pairs.

(Chap 2, Class-XII, New NCERT)

1.	Expenditure Method	–	Aggregate value of spending that the firms receive
2.	Income Method	–	Sum total of all factor payments
3.	Product Method	–	Aggregate value of final goods and services produced by firms

How many of the statements given above is/are correct?

(a) Only one
(b) Only two
(c) All three
(d) None of these

Ans. (c)

Exp. All the given pairs are correctly matched.

Expenditure method It is a method to calculate the national income.

When the income is being spent on the goods and services produced by the firms, it takes the form of aggregate expenditure received by the firms. In expenditure method, we can measure the uppermost flow by measuring the aggregate value spending that the firms receive for the final goods and services, which they produce.

Income method In this method of GDP estimation, sum of income earned by all factors of production in an economy is added. This method is based on the principle that all economic expenditures are equal to the total income generated by production of all economic goods and services.

Product method It is used to measure the aggregate value of final goods and services produced by all the firms.

30 Consider the following statements regarding Expenditure Method of GDP.

(Chap 2, Class-XII, New NCERT)
(Chap 2, Class-XII, Tamil Nadu Board)

1. This method looks at the supply side of the products.
2. In this method we add the final expenditures that each firm makes.

Which of the statements given above is/are correct?

(a) Only 1
(b) Only 2
(c) Both 1 and 2
(d) Neither 1 nor 2

Ans. (b)

Exp. Only statement (2) is correct regarding Expenditure Method of GDP. The expenditure method is a technique for measuring a country's Gross Domestic Product (GDP) by incorporating imports, exports, investments, consumption and government spending. The expenditure method can be regarded as the frequently used method to measure GDP.

According to the expenditure method, both private and public sector expenses incurred within a country's borders will give the total production value of finished goods and services over a time period. It gives the nominal GDP, which is then adjusted for inflation to arrive at the actual GDP.

Statement (1) is incorrect as GDP in expenditure method is calculated by looking at the demand side of products. It includes consumption expenditure made by households, government and foreign countries (Export and imports).

31 Consider the following statements.

(Chap 2, Class-XII, New NCERT)

1. CSO is a premier statistical institution for collecting data in India.
2. It presents the national income and estimates twice a year.

Which of the statements given above is/are correct?

(a) Only 1
(b) Only 2
(c) Both 1 and 2
(d) Neither 1 nor 2

Ans. (a)

Exp. Only statement (1) is correct as Central Statistical Organisation (CSO) is a premier statistical institution for collecting data in India. This organisation is under the administrative control of Ministry of Statistics and Programme Implementation (MoSPI).

Statement (2) is incorrect because it presents the national income and estimates annually.

Chapter 03

Economic Planning

Economic Planning

Planning in Indian Economy

Introduction

- Refers to the proces of creating a long-term vision and strategy for the country's economic development
- **Objective** For co-ordination of natural, economic and human resources; Balaced growth in socio-economic in different economic sectors

History of Planning in India

Visvesvaraya Plan

- Existence from 1934; M. Visvesvaraya formulated 10 year plan
- Emphasised on the increasing the industrial production

National Planning Committee

- Existence from 1938; Initiated by Netaji Subhash Chandra Bose; Chairman Jawaharlal Nehru

Gandhian Strategy

- Proposed by Acharya Shriman Narayan
- Emphasised on Economic Decentralisation

Bombay Plan

- Came in early 1944; Sir Purshottamdas Thakur Das, Mr. JRD Tata and six other attempted and published it
- Main Objective-Doubling Per Capita Income

Planning Commission

- Established in March 1950
- A Non-Constitutional Body
- Part of the Cabinet Organisation

National Development Council (NDC)

- Set-up on 6th August, 1952
- Also known as Rashtriya Vikas Parishad
- A Non-constitutional Body

NITI Aayog Plan

- Launched on 1st January, 2015 as National Institute for Transforming India (NITI) Aayog

Types of Planning

- **On the Basis of State and Market Inter-relation**
  - Imperative Planning
  - Indicative Planning
- **On the Basis of Process**
  - Centralised Planning
  - Decentralised
- **On the Basis of Area**
  - National Planning
  - Regional Planning
- **On the Basis of Result**
  - Structural Planning
  - Functional Planning
- **On the Basis of Duration**
  - Perspective Planning
  - Rolling Planning
  - Short-term Planning

Five Year Plan in India and its Abolition

Five Year Plans in India

- **First (1951-1956)** Based on Harrod Domar Model; Main focus on agricultural development
- **Second (1956-1961)** Based on PC Mahalanobis Model; Main focus on industrial development
- **Third (1961-1966)** Also called Gadgil Yojana; Main focus to make economy independent
- **Plan Holidays (1966-1969)** Government announced three annual plans from (1966-1969); To increase the exports in country
- **Fourth (1969-74)** Growth with stability; 14 major banks were nationalised
- **Fifth (1974-78)** Focuses on Garibi Hatao; A Twenty Point Programme (TPP) was launched in 1975
- **Rolling Plan (1978-80)** Brought out by Janata Party in 1978
  - The focus was enlargement of the employment potential in agriculture and allied activities
- **Sixth (1980-1985)** Emphasis on efficiency and monitoring of various schemes
  - Removal of poverty for both agriculture and industry
  - Economic reform announced (1991).
- **Seventh (1985-1990)** Establishment of a self-sufficient economy; Opportunities for productive employment and upgradation of technology
- **Annual Plan (1990-1992)** Two annual programmes were formed for the year. (1990-91) and (1991-92)
- **Eight (1992-1997)** Top priority was given to the development of Human Resources; Narasimha Rao launched the new Economic Policy; High growth rate was achieved
- **Ninth (1997-2007)** Focus was 'growth with social justice and inequality'; Failed to achieve the growth target of 6.5%
- **Tenth (2002-2007)** Aimed to double the Per Capita Income of India in next 10 years; Growth target was 8.0% but achieved only 7.6%
- **Eleventh (2007-12)** Prepared by C. Rangarajan; Theme was 'Rapid and Inclusive Growth'; Achieved a growth rate of 8%
- **Twelfth (2012-17)** Theme is Faster More Inclusive and Sustainable Growth; Target was 8% but achieved only 7.1% approx
- **Abolition of Five Year Plans** NITI Aayog replaced the Planning Commission; 15 Years Vision document in place of 5 Year Plan
  - 2017-18 to 2032-33 (Vision document); 2017-18 to 2024-25 (National Development Agency)
  - 2017-18 to 2019-20 (Three Year Action Agenda)

SOURCE *Old NCERT Class IX & X (The State and Economic Development), New NCERT Class XI (Indian Economy) Tamil Nadu Board Class XI (Consumption Analysis)*

Planning in Indian Economy

1 Consider the following statements.

(Chap 5, Class-IX & X, Old NCERT)

1. In 1951, the Planning Commission was set up with the Prime Minister as its Chairperson.
2. The goals of the Five Year Plans were growth, modernisation, self-reliance and equity.

Which of the statements given above is/are incorrect?

(a) Only 1 (b) Only 2
(c) Both 1 and 2 (d) Neither 1 nor 2

Ans. (a)

Exp. Statement (1) is incorrect because the Planning Commission was set up in 1950 with the Prime Minister as its Chairperson. After the Constitution of Planning Commission, the era of Five Year Plans began.

2 Consider the following statements regarding the important features pertaining to the objectives of planning in India. *(Chap 2, Class-XI, New NCERT)*

1. 'Economic and social planning' is a center subject.
2. The Constitution includes provisions for promoting co-operation on a voluntary basis between the union and the states.
3. The Constitution also sets out in broad outline the pattern of the welfare state envisaged and the fundamental principles on which it should rest.

Which of the following statements given above is/are correct?

(a) Only 1 (b) 2 and 3 (c) Only 3 (d) 1 and 2

Ans. (b)

Exp. Only statements (2) and (3) are correct regarding the important features pertaining to the objectives of planning in India.

The Constitution vests power in the union to ensure co-ordinated development while preserving the initiative and authority of the states in the spheres allotted to them.

Statement (1) is incorrect becuase Economic and social planning is concurrent subject. Both the Parliament and State Legislature can make laws on the subject is in Concurrent List.

3 Consider the following statements with respect to the objective of planning.

(Chap 5, Class-IX & X, Old NCERT)

1. To achieve steady and controlled growth in the economy.
2. To control and coordinate the system for the purpose of better allocation of the resources of the country.

Which of the statements given above is/are correct?

(a) Only 1 (b) Only 2
(c) Both 1 and 2 (d) Neither 1 nor 2

Ans. (c)

Exp. Both the statements (1) and (2) are correct with respect to the objective of planning.

The objective of the planning is to achieve steady and controlled growth in the economy. In economics, growth refers to increase in the country's capacity to produce the output of goods and services within the country.

The other objective of planning is to control and coordinate the system for the better allocation of resources of the country.

4 With reference to Prasanta Chandra Mahalanobis, which of the given statements are incorrect?

(Chap 2, Class-XI, New NCERT)

1. He is considered as the architect of Planning in India.
2. The Second Five Year Plan was based on his ideas.
3. He established the Indian Statistical Institute (ISI) in New Delhi.

Codes

(a) 1 and 2 (b) 2 and 3
(c) Only 3 (d) 1, 2 and 3

Ans. (c)

Exp. Statement (3) is incorrect as PC Mahalanobis established the Indian Statistical Institute (ISI) at Calcutta (not New Delhi) and he also started a journal 'Sankhya', which still serves as a respected forum for statisticians to discuss their ideas.

5 Consider the following statements with respect to planning and self-reliance. *(Chap 2, Class-XI, New NCERT)*

1. A nation can promote economic growth and modernisation by using its own resources or by using resources imported from other nations.
2. The first Seven Five Year Plans gave importance to self-reliance, which means avoiding imports of those goods, which could be produced in India itself.

Which of the statements given above is/are correct?

(a) Only 1 (b) Only 2
(c) Both 1 and 2 (d) Neither 1 nor 2

Ans. (c)

Exp. Both the statements (1) and (2) are correct with respect to planning and self-reliance. Self-reliance was one of the main objective of Five Year Plans.

Self-reliance means that a nation can promote economic growth and modernisation by using its own resources or by using resources imported from other nations.

The first Seven Five Year Plans gave importance to self-reliance which means avoiding imports of those goods which could be produced in India itself. The policy of self-reliance was considered a necessity in order to reduce our dependence on foreign countries, especially for food.

Five Years' Plans

6 With reference to the 'Perspective Plan' which of the following statements is/are incorrect? *(Chap 2, Class-XI, New NCERT)*

1. It was part of Indian economic planning till 2017 and specified the objectives to be attained in the period of twenty years.
2. Contrary to the Five Year Plans, it gave equal importance to all sectors of the economy.

Codes

(a) Only 1 (b) Only 2
(c) Both 1 and 2 (d) Neither 1 nor 2

Ans. (b)

Exp. Statement (2) is incorrect because in economy, different sectors are competing with each other for limited resources. Further the objectives of planning *viz* growth, modernisation, self-reliance, etc are itself contradictory. It resulted in the government giving more emphasis to some particular sector.

7 Which of the following is in the correct order in terms of its incorporation? *(Chap 2, Class XI, Old NCERT)*

(a) Bombay Plan > Gandhian Plan > People's Plan > Sarvodaya Plan
(b) People's Plan > Sarvodaya Plan > Bombay Plan > Gandhian Plan
(c) Sarvodaya Plan > Bombay Plan > Gandhian Plan > People's Plan
(d) Gandhian Plan > Sarvodaya Plan > Bombay Plan > People's Plan

Ans. (a)

Exp. The correct order is Bombay Plan > Gandhian Plan > People's Plan > Sarvodaya Plan.

Bombay Plan It was presented by 8 leading industrialists of Bombay, Purshotamdas Thakurdas, JRD Tata, GD Birla, Lala Sri Ram, Kasturbhai Lalbhai, AD Shroff, Ardeshir Dalal and John Mathai in January, 1944.

Gandhian Plan Sriman Narayan Agarwal formulated 'Gandhian Plan' in 1944.

People Plan This plan was formulated by MN Roy in 1945. The plan was based on Marxist socialism and advocated the need of providing the people with the 'basic necessities of life'. Agricultural and industrial sectors, both were equally highlighted by the plan.

Jaiprakash Narayan designed the **Sarvodaya Plan** in 1950. This plan was inspired by Vinoba Bhave's Sarvodaya Idea and Gandhian Plan. Agriculture and small and cottage enterprises were highlighted in this plan.

8 Consider the following statements with respect to Gandhian plan. *(Chap 2, Class-XI, Old NCERT)*

1. The plan articulated a 'decentralised economic structure' for India with 'self-contained villages'.
2. Jayaprakash Narayan and Jawaharlal Nehru formulated the Gandhian plan.

Which of the above statements is/are incorrect?

(a) Only 1
(b) Only 2
(c) Both 1 and 2
(d) Neither 1 nor 2

Ans. (b)

Exp. Statement (2) is incorrect as Gandhian plan was formulated by Acharya Shriman Narayan Agarwal in 1944.

9 Consider the following pairs. *(Chap 2, Class-XI, New NCERT)*

Plans	Objectives
1. First Plan	Community development projects
2. Second Plan	Heavy industries
3. Third Plan	Green revolution

How many of the above pairs is/are correctly matched?

(a) Only one pair
(b) Only two pairs
(c) All three pairs
(d) None of the pairs

Ans. (c)

Exp. All three pairs are correctly matched.

First Five Year Plan gave preference to agriculture and related community development programme.

The main objectives of the Second Plan was an increase of 25 percent in real national income, a large expansion of employment opportunities; rapid industrialisation; and reduction of economic inequalities.

In the Third Five Year Plan, 1961-1966, the concept of the green revolution was formulated.

10 Consider the following statements. *(Chap 2, Class-XI, New NCERT)*

1. The Second Five Year Plan (FYP) was largely based on the Mahalanobis ideas and hence was called 'Mahalanobis Plan'.
2. Mahalanobis is also credited with the achievement of publishing journal 'Sankhya'?

Which of the statements given above is/are correct?

(a) Only 1
(b) Only 2
(c) Both 1 and 2
(d) Neither 1 nor 2

Ans. (c)

Exp. Both the statements (1) and (2) are correct as Five-Year Plans (FYPs) are centralised and integrated national economic programs in India. The Second Five Year Plan (1956-1961) was based on the ideas of Mahalanobis. The Second Plan focused on the development of the public sector and 'Rapid Industrialisation'. Mahalanobis established the Indian Statistical Institute (ISI) in Calcutta and started a journal, Sakhya which still serves as a respective forum for statisticians to discuss their ideas.

11 **Consider the following statements with respect to the Seventh Five Year Plan.** *(Chap 2, Class-XI, New NCERT)*

1. The proportion of GDP contributed by the industrial sector increased from 13% in 1950-1951 to 24.6% in 1990-1991.
2. However, Indian industry was restricted to cotton textiles and jute.

Which of the statements given above is/are incorrect?

(a) Only 1 (b) Only 2
(c) Both 1 and 2 (d) Neither 1 nor 2

Ans. (b)

Exp. Statement (2) is incorrect because during Seventh Five Year Plan, Indian industry was not restricted only to cotton textiles and jute but to other industrial sector also. It became well diversified by 1990.

12 **Which of the following statements is not one of the outcomes of the first Seven Five Year Plans?** *(Chap 2, Class-XI, New NCERT)*

(a) India became self-sufficient in food production.
(b) Land reforms resulted in abolition of the hated zamindari system.
(c) In the industrial sector, the performance of public sector enterprises was satisfactory.
(d) Excessive government regulation prevented growth of entrepreneurship.

Ans. (c)

Exp. Statement (c) is not considered as the outcome of the first Seven Five Year Plans.

Inspite of the contribution made by the public sector to the growth of Indian economy, some economists were concerned about the performance of many public sector enterprises, during first Seven Five Years Plan. It was because after four decades of planned development, no distinction was made between the individual potential of the public and the private sector.

13 **In the context of India's Five Year Plans, a shift in pattern of industrialisation with lower emphasis on the heavy industry and move on infrastructure began in** *(Chap 5, Class IX & X, Old NCERT), (IAS Pre 2010)*

(a) Fourth Plan (b) Sixth Plan
(c) Eighth Plan (d) Tenth Plan

Ans. (c)

Exp. The Eighth Five Year Plan witnessed a shift in pattern of industrialisation with lower emphasis on the heavy industry and move on infrastructure. It was operationalised between 1992 and 1997.

14 **Consider the following statements.** *(Chap 2, Class-XI, New NCERT)*

Statement-I The Plan Holiday was declared for three years as there was discontinuity in the planning process.

Statement-II Plan period was from 1965-1968.

Which one of the following is correct in respect of the above statements?

(a) Both Statement-I and Statement-II are correct and Statement-II is the correct explanation for Statement-I.
(b) Both Statement-I and Statement-II are correct and Statement-II is not the correct explanation for Statement-I.
(c) Statement-I is correct but Statement-II is incorrect
(d) Statement-I is incorrect but Statement-II is correct

Ans. (c)

Exp. Statement-I is correct but Statement-II is incorrect. The Plan Holiday is also called Gadgil Yojana. The main target of this plan was to make the economy independent. The stress was laid on agriculture and the improvement in the production of wheat. Plan Holiday was developed due to the failure of the Third Five Year Plan. The main reason behind the failure of the Third Five Year Plan was the Indo-Pakistani War (1965) and the Sino-India War(1962) leading to plan holiday. However, there were three annual plans between 1966 and 1969.

15 **The Eleventh Five Year Plan strategy to raise agricultural output envisage which of the following?** *(Chap 2, Class-XI, New NCERT)*

1. Greater attention to land reforms.
2. Double the rate of growth of irrigated area.
3. Promote animal husbandry and fishery.
4. Interest free credit to the farmers.

Codes

(a) 1 and 3 (b) 2 and 3 (c) 1, 2 and 3 (d) 2 and 4

Ans. (c)

Exp. The 11th Five Year Plan strategy to raise agricultural output envisages i.e., Greater attention to land reform, Double the rate of growth of irrigated area, Promote animal husbandary and fishery. 11th Five Year Plan (2007-2012) was prepared by the C. Rangarajan. Its main theme was 'Rapid and inclusive growth', achieved a growth rate of 8% against a target of 9% growth.

16 **The Twelfth Five Year Plan focussed on inclusive growth. Which of the following were considered as challenges for inclusiv4eness?** *(Chap 2, Class-XI, New NCERT)*

1. Poverty
2. Group inequality
3. Regional imbalance
4. Unemployment

Codes

(a) 1, 3 and 4 (b) 1, 2, 3 and 4 (c) 1, 2 and 4 (d) 2 and 3

Ans. (b)

Exp. All of the above mentioned options were considered as challenges for inclusiveness. The Twelfth Five Year (2012-2017) Plan focussed on inclusive growth. This plan aimed to doubled the per capita income of India in the next 10 years. It also aimed to reduce the poverty ratio of 15% by 2012. Its growth target was 8.0% but it achieved only 7.6%. The slogan of the Twelfth Plan is 'Faster, More Sustainable, and More Inclusive Growth'.

Chapter 04

Demography, Poverty and Unemployment

Demography, Poverty and Unemployment

Demography

Introduction

- Statistical study of human population, is known as Demography
- **Birth rate** The number of live birth per 1000 population
- **Death rate** The number of death per 1000 population
- **Crude death rate** The mortality rate from all causes of death
- **Infant mortality rate** The number of death of infants under age 1 per 1000 live birth
- **Density** Number of persons per sq/km

Population Census

- First census in 1799 (Sweden)
- First census in India started from 1881 (Lord Ripon)
- 15th census in 2011 (7th after Independent India)

Population Expansion

- Stationary phase (1901-1921)
- Steady phase (1921-1951)
- Population explosion (1951-1981)
- Declining of population (1981-2011)

Demographic Composition

- Density of population
- Literacy
- Ethnic composition
- Linguistic composition

Poverty

Introduction

- It is defined by calorie intake
- Major type of poverty
- **Absolute poverty** Severe deprivation of basic human needs

Relative poverty Economic inequality in location or society in which people live

Poverty Estimation in India

- **Minimum Calorie Consumption** - Food with 2400 calorie (rural person) and 2100 calorie (urban person)
- **Monthly per capita income**
- Based on expenditure on food and some goods
- **Head Count Ratio** (HCR)
- Proportion of population existing below poverty line

Poverty Related Committee

Committee	Formation
YK Alag Committee	1979
Lokadawala Committee	1989
Tendulkar Committee	2004
Rangarajan Committee	2012

Unemployment

Introduction

- Occurs when a person who is actively searching for employment is unable to find work
- Problem of unemploy gives rise to the problem of poverty
- **Types Involuntary**
  - **Structural** Mismatch in skills and demand for labour
  - **Frictional** Unemployment between job
  - **Seasonal** Unemployment due to different season
  - **Cyclical** Unemployment that rises during downturn and falls
- **Voluntary** Not being able to find employment of his/her own choice

Causes

- Population Growth
- Mobility of Labour
- Education
- Agriculture
- Lack of Skills
- Poor Industrialisation
- Lack of Investment

SOURCE **New NCERT Class IX** *(People as a Resource)*, **New NCERT Class IX** *(Poverty as a Challenge)*, **Old NCERT Class IX&X** *(An Overview of the Indian Economy)*, **New NCERT Class X** *(Sectors of Indian Economy)*, **New NCERT Class X** *(Development)*, **New NCERT Class X** *(Food Security in India)*, **New NCERT Class XI** *(Indian Economy on the Eve of Independence Poverty)*, **New NCERT Class XI** *(Employment : Growth, Information and Other Issues)*, **New NCERT Class XI** *(Poverty)*, **New NCERT Class XI** *(Comparative Analysis of India and Its Neighbouring Countries)*

Demography

1 Consider the following statements.

(Chap 2 Class-IX, New NCERT)

1. Registrar General and Census Commissioner of India conducts demographic survey of India including Census of India and Linguistic Survey of India.
2. The position of Registrar is usually held by a civil servant holding the rank of joint secretary.
3. The first census of India was conducted in the year 1872 but the first decennial census took place in 1881.

How many of the statements given above is/are correct?
(a) Only one (b) Only two (c) All three (d) None of these

***Ans.* (c)**

Exp. All three statements i.e. (1), (2) and (3) are true as Registrar General and Census Commissioner of India conducts demographic survey of India Including Census of India and Linguistic Survey of India. It was established in the year 1961. The position of Registrar is usually held by a civil servant holding the rank of joint secretary. The department comes under the Ministry of Home Affairs.

The first census of India was conducted in the year 1872 under the rule of Lord Mayo but the first decennial census took place in 1881 under Lord Ripon. It was called the first synchronised census.

2 With reference to demography of India, which of the following statements is/are correct?

(Chap 1, Class-XI, New NCERT)

1. The second stage of demographic transition began after 1921.
2. The overall literacy level was less than 16% at the time of independence.

Select the correct answer using the codes given below.
(a) Only 1 (b) Only 2
(c) Both 1 and 2 (d) Neither 1 nor 2

***Ans.* (c)**

Exp. Both the statements (1) and (2) are correct. Regarding demography of India. The second stage of demographic transition began after 1921. The year 1921 is often related as the year of great divide; the last period in which India's population declined. The overall literacy rate was less than 16% at the time of independence. Out of this, the female literacy rate was about 7% at a negligible low rate.

3 Identify the incorrect statement.

(Chap 2, Class-IX, New NCERT)

(a) Birth rate is the number of babies born for every 1,000 people during a particular period of time.
(b) Death rate is the number of people per 1,000 who die during a particular period of time.
(c) The literacy rates have increased from 18% in 1951 to 74% in 2011.
(d) None of the above

***Ans.* (d)**

Exp. None of the given statements are incorrect.

Birth rate is the number of babies born for every 1,000 people during a particular period of time. As per 2020 estimate, the birth rate in India is 18.2 births per thousand population.

Death rate is the number of people per 1,000 who die during a particular period of time. As per 2020 estimate, death rate in India is 7.3 deaths per thousand population.

The literacy rates have increased from 18.32% in 1951 to 74.04% in 2011. It was highest in Kerala and lowest in Bihar. Lakshadweep is the most literate Union Territory of India.

4 Consider the following statements.

(Chap 1 Class-X, New NCERT)

Statement-I Crude Death Rate is the mortality rate from all causes of death for a population.

Statement-II It is in terms of number of deaths in a particular month per thousand of population in a particular region.

Which one of the following is correct in respect of the above statements?
(a) Both Statement-I and Statement-II are correct and Statement-II is the correct explanation for Statement-I.
(b) Both Statement-I and Statement-II are correct and Statement-II is not the correct explanation for Statement-I.
(c) Statement-I is correct but Statement-II is incorrect.
(d) Statement-I is incorrect but Statement-II is correct.

***Ans.* (c)**

Exp. Statement-I is correct but Statement-II is incorrect. The Crude Death Rate is defined as "the mortality rate from all causes of death for a population."

Crude Death Rate the total number of deaths to residents in a specified geographic area (country, state, etc.) divided by the total population for the same geographic area for a specified time period, (usually a calendar year and multiplied by 1,000.

5 Consider the following statements with respect to literacy rate in India. *(Chap 2, Class-IX, New NCERT)*

1. Literacy among males is nearly 14.4% higher than females.
2. It is about 4.2% higher in urban areas as compared to rural areas.

Which of the statements given above is/are correct?
(a) Only 1 (b) Only 2
(c) Both 1 and 2 (d) Neither 1 nor 2

***Ans.* (a)**

Exp. Only statement (1) is correct with respect to literacy rate in India. Literacy rate among males is nearly 14.4% higher than females.

Statement (2) is incorrect because in urban areas literacy rate is about 14.2% and not 4.2% higher as compared to rural areas.

6 **Arrange the following states in descending order according to density of population in 2011 and select the correct answer using the codes given below.**

(Chap 1, Class-X, New NCERT)

1. Kerala
2. Bihar
3. West Bengal
4. Uttar Pradesh

Codes

(a) 1, 2, 3, 4 (b) 2, 3, 1, 4
(c) 3, 2, 1, 4 (d) None of these

Ans. (b)

Exp. The correct descending order according to density of population is Bihar (1106 person/sq km), West Bengal (1,028 person/sq km), Kerala, (860 person/sq km), Uttar Pradesh (829 person/sq km), as per Census 2011.

The population density of India in 2011 was 382 per sq km. Among the states, Bihar is on the top of the list with a population density of 1102 person/sq km. The lowest population density among the states is found in Arunachal Pradesh, 17 person/sq km.

7 **Consider the following Assertion (A) and Reason (R) and choose the correct code.**

(Chap 2, Class-IX, New NCERT)

Assertion (A) The quality of the population ultimately decides the growth rate of the country.

Reason (R) The quality of population depends upon the literacy rate, health of a person indicated by life expectancy and skill formation acquired by the people of the country.

Codes

(a) Both A and R are true and R is the correct explanation of A.
(b) Both A and R are true, but R is not the correct explanation of A.
(c) A is true, but R is false.
(d) A is false, but R is true.

Ans. (a)

Exp. Both Assertion (A) and Reason (R) are true and Reason (R) is the correct explanation of Assertion (A).

The quality of population determines capability of human resource of a country in ensuring the productivity, standard of living and social activities.

The factors that check quality of population can be education, health, sanitation etc. Literate and healthy persons are an asset for the country.

8 **Arrange the following religious groups in increasing order of their population in India.**

(Chap 1, Class-IX, New NCERT)

1. Muslims
2. Buddhists
3. Sikhs
4. Jains
5. Christians

Codes

(a) 4, 2, 3, 5, 1 (b) 4, 2, 1, 3, 5
(c) 2, 4, 3, 5, 1 (d) 2, 3, 4, 1, 5

Ans. (a)

Exp. The religious groups in increasing order of their population in India are Jains, Buddhists, Sikhs, Christians and Muslims.

As per Census 2011 the total population is 121.09 crores, Hindu 96.63 crores (79.8%), Muslim 17.22 crores (14.2%), Christian 2.78 crores (2.3%), Sikh 2.08 crores (1.7%), Buddhist 0.84 crores (0.7%), Jain 0.45 crores (0.4%) other religious and persuasion (ORP) 0.79 crores (0.7%) and religion not stated 0.29 crores (0.2%).

The growth rate of population in the decade 2001-2011 was 17.7%. The growth rate of population of the different religious communities in the same period was Hindu 16.8%, Muslim 24.6%, Christian (15.5%), Sikh (8.4%), Buddhist (6.1%) and Jain (5.4%).

9 **Consider the following statements with reference to demography of India.** *(Chap 1, Class-XI, New NCERT)*

1. Life expectancy has increased from 32 years to 69 years from 1947 to 2020.
2. The Infant Mortality Rate has been reduced by around 6 times from independence till date.

Which of the statement(s) given above is/are correct?

(a) Only 1 (b) Only 2
(c) Both 1 and 2 (d) Neither 1 nor 2

Ans. (c)

Exp. Both the statements (1) and (2) are correct with reference to demography of India.

In India, life expectancy has increased from 32 years to 69 years from 1947 to 2020.

Life expectancy refers to the number of years an individual is expected to live based on statistical average.

Infant Mortality Rate is the number of deaths per 1,000 live births of children under one year of age. Infant Mortality Rate in India by the year 2020 was around 30 per 1000 live births.

Poverty

10 **The Gupta family lives in a rural village in India. They own a small plot of land but often struggle to grow enough food to feed themselves. They lack access to clean water and sanitation facilities.**

(Chap 4 Class-XI, New NCERT)

Which type of poverty Gupta family faces?

(a) Relative Poverty (b) Situational Poverty
(c) Absolute Poverty (d) Chronic Poverty

Ans. (c)

Exp. Gupta family faces Absolute poverty. Absolute poverty is a condition characterised by severe deprivation of basic human needs including food, safe drinking water, sanitation facilities, health, shelter, education and information.

It does not include a broader quality of life issues or overall level of inequality in society. It does not recognise important social and cultural needs of an individual.

11 **Which of the following factors contribute to poverty in India?** *(Chap 3, Class-IX, New NCERT)*

1. Landlessness
2. Unemployment
3. Size of families
4. Illiteracy

Codes

(a) 1 and 4 (b) 1, 2 and 3 (c) 1 and 2 (d) 1, 2, 3 and 4

Ans. (d)

Exp. Landlessness, unemployment, size of families, illiteracy, social exclusion, lack of infrastructure, etc., are the factors that contribute to poverty in India. It is illiteracy and not literacy, which contribute to poverty in India.

A large number of rural poor are either landless or small farmers having small holding and the income from these small holdings is not sufficient to meet the family's basic requirements.

Unemployment or underemployment and the casual and intermittent nature of work in both urban and rural areas cause poverty. Larger the size of family, larger will be the expenditure, which ultimately results into poverty.

12 **Which of the following statements is/are incorrect regarding poverty?** *(Chap 3, Class-IX, New NCERT)*

(a) A person is considered poor if his or her income or consumption level falls below a given 'minimum level' necessary to fulfill the basic needs.
(b) A common method used to measure poverty is based on the income or consumption level.
(c) Poverty line does not vary with time and place.
(d) None of the above

Ans. (c)

Exp. Statement (c) is incorrect regarding poverty because poverty line may vary with time and place as what is necessary to satisfy the basic needs is different at different times and in different countries.

Therefore, each country uses an imaginary line that is considered appropriate for its existing level of development and its accepted minimum social norms.

13 **Consider the following statements about vulnerability in context of poverty.** *(Chap 3, Class-IX, New NCERT)*

1. Vulnerability to poverty is a measure, which describes the lesser probability of certain communities or individuals of becoming, or remaining, poor in the coming years.
2. Vulnerability is determined by the options available to different communities for finding an alternative mode of living in terms of assets, education, health and job opportunities.

Which of the statements given above is/are incorrect?

(a) Only 1 (b) Only 2
(c) Both 1 and 2 (d) Neither 1 nor 2

Ans. (a)

Exp. Only statement (1) is incorrect about vulnerability. Vulnerability to poverty is a measure, which describes the greater (not lesser) probability of certain communities (e.g., Backward class) or individuals (e.g., widow or a physically handicapped person) of becoming or remaining poor in the coming years.

14 **Consider the following statements.** *(Chap 3, Class-IX, New NCERT)*

1. To determine the poverty line in India, a minimum level of food requirement, clothing, footwear, fuel and light, educational and medical requirement, etc., are determined for subsistence.
2. The present formula for food requirement while estimating the poverty line is based on the desired daily expenditure.

Which of the statements given above is/are incorrect?

(a) Only 1
(b) Only 2
(c) Both 1 and 2
(d) Neither 1 nor 2

Ans. (b)

Exp. Only statement (2) is incorrect because the present formula for food requirement while estimating the poverty line is based on the desired calorie requirement (not desired daily expenditure).

Food items, such as, cereals, pulses, vegetable, milk, oil, sugar, etc., together provide these needed calories. The calorie needs vary depending on age, sex and the type of work a person does.

15 **Which of the following statements is/are incorrect regarding poverty estimation?** *(Chap 3, Class-IX, New NCERT)*

(a) Despite less calorie requirement, the higher amount for urban areas has been fixed because of high prices of many essential products in urban centres.
(b) The poverty line is estimated periodically by conducting sample surveys by the Central Statistical Organisation (CSO).
(c) For making comparisons between developing countries, the World Bank uses a uniform standard for the poverty line.
(d) None of the above

Ans. (b)

Exp. Statement (b) is incorrect regarding poverty estimation. The poverty line is estimated periodically by conducting sample surveys. These surveys are conducted by National Sample Survey Organisation (NSSO) normally in every five years.

In 2019, NSSO was merged with Central Statistical Organisation (CSO) to constitute a unified body called National Statistical Office (NSO).

For the year 2011-12, the poverty line for a person was fixed at ₹ 972 per month for rural areas and ₹ 1407 for urban areas as per rangarajan committee report.

16 With reference to the poverty line in India, consider the following statements. *(Chap 4, Class-XI New NCERT)*

1. For the year 2011-12, the poverty line for a person was fixed at ₹ 1000 per month for rural areas and ₹ 816 for urban areas.
2. Based on the Tendulkar poverty line, for 2011-12 the number of poor in the country was pegged at 21.9% of the population.

Which of the statements given above is/are correct?

(a) Only 1
(b) Only 2
(c) Both 1 and 2
(d) Neither 1 nor 2

Ans. (d)

Exp. Neither statement (1) nor (2) is correct. In the year 2011-12, the poverty line for a person was fixed at ₹ 816 for rural areas and for urban areas it is ₹ 1000 under Tendulkar methodology. The poverty line of urban is quite high due to the high prices of goods and services in urban areas.

In 2011-12, the number of poor is 26.92 crore people. The percentage of persons below the poverty line in 2011-12 has been estimated as 25.7% in rural areas, 13.7% in urban areas and 21.9% for the country as a whole.

17 With reference to the poverty line in India, consider the following statements. *(Chap 4 Class-XI, New NCERT)*

1. While determining the poverty line, a minimum level of food requirement, clothing, footwear, fuel and light, educational and medical requirement, etc., are determined for subsistence.
2. The accepted average calories requirement in India is 2100 calories per person per day in rural areas and 2400 calories per person per day in urban areas.

Which of the statements given above is/are correct?

(a) Only 1
(b) Only 2
(c) Both 1 and 2
(d) Neither 1 nor 2

Ans. (a)

Exp. Only statement (1) is correct as while determining the poverty line in India, a minimum level of food requirement, clothing, footwear, fuel and light, educational and medical requirements, etc., are determined for subsistence. These physical quantities are multiplied by their prices in rupees and thereby the poverty line is arrived at.

Statement (2) is incorrect because the accepted average calorie requirement for defining the poverty line in India has been 2400 calories per person per day for rural areas and 2100 calories per person per day for urban areas.

18 Match the following lists and choose the correct code. *(Chap 4, Class-XI, New NCERT)*

List-I (Types of Poverty)	List-II (Features)
A. Chronic	1. Who are rich most of the time but sometimes have a bad luck.
B. Churning	2. Who regularly move in and out of poverty.
C. Occasionally	3. Who are always and usually poor.

Codes

	A	B	C		A	B	C
(a)	2	1	3	(b)	3	2	1
(c)	1	3	2	(d)	1	2	3

Ans. (b)

Exp. The correct matching is A-3, B-2, C-1.

Chronic Poverty These are such type of poor who are always poor and those who are usually poor but who may sometimes have a little more money e.g. casual workers.

Churning Poverty These are such group of poor who regularly move in and out of poverty e.g. small farmers and seasonal workers.

Occasionally Poverty These are such type of poor who are rich most of the time but may sometimes have a patch of bad luck. They are also called as transient poor.

19 Consider the following Assertion (A) and Reason (R) and choose the correct code. *(Chap 3, Class-IX, New NCERT)*

Assertion (A) Social exclusion is both a cause as well as a consequence of poverty.

Reason (R) Social exclusion is a process through which individuals or groups are excluded from facilities, benefits and opportunities that others enjoy.

Codes

(a) Both A and R are true and R is the correct explanation of A.
(b) Both A and R are true, but R is not the correct explanation of A.
(c) A is true, but R is false.
(d) A is false, but R is true.

Ans. (a)

Exp. Both Assertion (A) and Reason (R) are true and Reason (R) is the correct explanation of Assertion (A). Social exclusion is both a cause as well as a consequence of poverty.

Poverty must be seen in terms of the person living in poor surrounding with other poor people, excluded from enjoying social equality of better-off people in better surroundings.

Broadly, it is a process through which individuals or groups are excluded from facilities, benefits and opportunities that other enjoy.

20 Which of the following statements is incorrect about hunger? *(Chap 4, Class-IX, New NCERT)*

(a) Hunger is not just an expression of poverty, it brings about poverty.
(b) Chronic hunger is a consequence of diets persistently inadequate in terms of quantity and/or quality.
(c) Seasonal hunger is related to cycles of food growing and harvesting.
(d) The proportion of chronic hunger is higher than seasonal hunger.

Ans. (d)

Exp. Statement (d) is incorrect about hunger as the proportion of seasonal hunger is higher than the chronic hunger. Chronic hunger is a consequence of diets persistently inadequate in terms of quantity or quality. Poor people suffer from chronic hunger because of their low income and in turn inability to buy food even for survival.

On the other hand, seasonal hunger is related to cycles of food growing and harvesting. It is prevalent in rural areas because of seasonal nature of agricultural activities and in urban areas because of casual workers.

21 Which of the following statements is incorrect regarding vulnerable groups? *(Chap 3, Class-IX, New NCERT)*

(a) Social groups, which are most vulnerable to poverty, are Scheduled Castes and Scheduled Tribe households.
(b) Among the economic groups, the most vulnerable groups are the rural agricultural labour households.
(c) Although the average for people Below Poverty Line for all groups in India is 22 and 43 out of 100 people belong to the Other Backward Castes.
(d) None of the above

Ans. (c)

Exp. Statement (c) is incorrect regarding vulnerable groups as the average for people Below Poverty Line (BPL) for all groups in India is 22 and 43 out of 100 people belonging to Scheduled Tribes (not other Backward Castes) are not able to meet their basic need.

Some of the socially vulnerable groups are Scheduled Castes and Scheduled Tribes. On the other hand, some of the economically vulnerable groups are rural agricultural labourer, urban casual labours, etc.

22 Consider the following statements. *(Chap 4, Class-XI, New NCERT)*

1. Monetary value (per capita expenditure) of the minimum calorie intake has been used as a metric to determine official poverty line in India.
2. Government uses Monthly Per Capita Expenditure (MPCE) as proxy for income of households to identify the poor.
3. Before Independence, Dadabhai Naoroji thought for the first time about determining a poverty line.

How many of the above statements is/are correct?

(a) Only one (b) Only two
(c) All three (d) None of these

Ans. (c)

Exp. All three statements i.e., (1), (2) and (3) are correct as there are many ways of measuring poverty. One way is to determine it by the monetary value (per capita expenditure) of the minimum calorie intake that was estimated at 2,400 calories for a rural person and 2,100 for a person in the urban area. In India, the government uses Monthly Per Capita Expenditure (MPCE) as proxy for income of households to identify the poor.

In pre-independent India, Dadabhai Naoroji was the first to discuss the concept of a poverty line. He used the menu for a prisoner and used appropriate prevailing prices to arrive at what may be called 'jail cost of living'.

23 Consider the following pairs. *(Chap 4, Class-XI, New NCERT)*

	Committee	Poverty Line
1.	Y K Alagh	on the basis of nutritional requirement.
2.	Lakdawala	on the basis of basket of goods and services.
3.	Tendulkar	cost of living.

How many of the above pairs is/are correctly matched?

(a) Only one pair (b) Only two pairs
(c) All three pairs (d) None of these

Ans. (c)

Exp. All three pairs i.e. (1), (2) and (3) are correctly matched.

Alagh Committee (1979) constituted by the Planning Commission under the chairmanship of YK Alagh, constructed a poverty line for rural and urban areas on the basis of nutritional requirements and related consumption expenditure.

Lakdawala Committee (1993) Task Force chaired by DT Lakdawala, based on the assumption that the basket of goods and services used to calculate Consumer Price Index-Industrial Workers (CPI-IW) and Consumer Price Index- Agricultural Labourers (CPI-AL) reflect the consumption patterns of the poor.

Tendulkar Committee (2005) It was constituted by the Planning Commission. The committee adopted the poverty line on the basis of cost of living and found that all India poverty line (2004-05) was ₹ 446.68 per capita per month in rural areas ₹ 578.80 per capita per month in urban areas.

24 Which of the following methods has/have been used to estimate poverty in India? *(Chap 3, Class-IX, New NCERT) (UPPSC Pre 2020)*

1. Head Count Ratio 2. Calorie intake
3. Household Consumption Expenditure
4. Per Capita Income

Select the correct answer from the codes given below.

(a) 2 and 3 (b) 1, 2 and 3 (c) Only 3 (d) 1, 2, 3 and 4

Ans. (b)

Exp. Head Count Ratio, Calorie intake and House hold Consumption Expenditure are the methods which have been used to estimate Poverty in India. The Head Count Ratio (HCR) is the population proportion that survives or lives, lower than the poverty threshold. It disregards the depth of poverty, if the poor become poorer, the head count index does not change.

The Planning Commission has drawn out the basic line of calorie intake for the rural and urban people of India. Household consumption expenditure is used to estimate poverty in India. If the income or consumption falls below a given minimum level then the household is said to be Below the Poverty Line (BPL).

25 Which of the following economic factors may have contributed to the cause of poverty in India? *(Chap 3, Class-IX, New NCERT)*

1. Low capital formation 2. Lack of infrastructure
3. Lack of demand 4. Pressure of population
5. Lack of social/welfare nets

Codes

(a) 1, 2 and 3 (b) 1, 2 and 4 (c) 2, 3 and 4 (d) All of these

Ans. (d)

Exp. All of the above mentioned factors contributed to the cause of poverty in India.

Causes of Poverty in India

1. **Low capital formation and Lack of Infrastructure** Lack of investment results in low capital formation where the country will not have enough money to develop infrastructure like roads, bridges, railways, industries and machinery leads to capital deficiency. It reflects lower production in the nation, resulting in fewer jobs and therefore, lower income levels.
2. **Lack of Demand** Economic development has been low in India. There is a gap between the requirement and the availability of goods and services.
3. **Pressure of population** Rapid population growth reduces per capita income growth and well-being, which tends to increase poverty. In densely populated poor nations with pressure on land, rapid population growth increases landlessness and hence the incidence of poverty.
4. **Lack of social welfare net** Apart from economic factors, there are also social factors hindering the eradication of poverty in India. Some of the hindrances in this regard are the laws of inheritance, caste system, certain traditions, etc.

26 Consider the following statements. *(Chap 3, Class-IX, New NCERT)*

1. Uttar Pradesh and Odisha continue to be the two poorest states with poverty ratios of 33.7 and 32.6% respectively.
2. The reason for higher poverty rate in Odisha, Madhya Pradesh, Bihar and Uttar Pradesh is rural poverty.

Which of the statements given above is/are incorrect?

(a) Only 1 (b) Only 2
(c) Both 1 and 2 (d) Neither 1 nor 2

Ans. (c)

Exp. Both the statements (1) and (2) are incorrect.

As per Census 2011, Bihar (not Uttar Pradesh) and Odisha continue to be the two poorest states with poverty ratio of 33.7 and 32.6% respectively.

Along with rural poverty, urban poverty is also high in Odisha, Madhya Pradesh, Bihar and Uttar Pradesh. As per Census 2011, the poverty ratio in states such as Odisha, Madhya Pradesh, Bihar and Uttar Pradesh are 32.6%, 31.7%, 33.7% and 29.4% respectively.

27 Consider the following statements regarding Gini coefficient. *(Chap 6, Class-XI, New NCERT)*

1. It is an index for the degree of inequality in the distribution of income/wealth.
2. It lies 0 and 1 with 0 represents perfect equality and 1 indicates absolute inequality.
3. It was developed by Italian statistician Carrado Gini in 1912.

How many of the statements given above is/are correct?

(a) Only one (b) Only two
(c) All three (d) None of these

Ans. (c)

Exp. All three statements i.e. (1), (2) and (3) are correct regarding Gini Coefficient. The Gini Index is a measure of the distribution of income across a population. It measures inequality on a scale from 0 to 1, where higher values indicate higher inequality.

This can sometimes be shown as a percentage from 0 to 100%, this is then called the 'Gini Index'. It was developed by Italian statistician Corrado Gini in 1912 .

28 A Lorenz curve dips sharply in the initial stage and then plateaus. What does this suggest about the income distribution in that country? *(Chap 6, Class-XI, New NCERT)*

(a) A small number of individuals possess a significant portion of the income.
(b) Income distribution is relatively equal amongst most of the population.
(c) Poverty is widespread and significant across all income levels.
(d) The data used to construct the curve is likely inaccurate or unreliable.

Ans. (a)

Exp. Statements (a) is correct with reference relating between Lorenz Curve and Income distribution. Where in Lorenz Curve dipping sharply in the initial stage and then getting plateaus.

Thus the sharp initial dip indicates a high concentration of income in the hands of a few, while the plateau shows lesser disparity among the remaining population.

The Lorenz curve is a graphical distribution of wealth developed by Max Lorenz in 1906, shows the proportion of income earned by any given percentage of the population. The line at the 45° angle shows perfectly equal income distribution, while other line shows the actual distribution of income.

29 Consider the following statements.

(Chap 4, Class-XI, New NCERT)

1. Poverty can be caused due to social, economic, and political inequality.
2. Aggregate poverty is just the sum of individual poverty.
3. A large section of the rural poor in India are the small farmers.

How many of the above statements is/are correct?

(a) Only one (b) Only two
(c) All three (d) None of these

Ans. (c)

Exp. All three statements i.e. (1), (2) and (3) are correct as poverty is a socio-economic condition that is the result of multiple factors not just income. These factors include race, sexual identity, sexual orientation, and little to no access to education, among others. Aggregate poverty is just the sum of individual poverty.

Agriculture remains the primary source of income for India's population, and the majority of India's farmers subsist on small farms, less than two hectares (five acres).

30 Which of the following factors are not responsible for poverty? *(Chap 3, Class-IX, New NCERT)*

1. Inflation
2. Increase in government expenditure
3. Deficit financing
4. Short shavings and capital formation

Select the correct answer using the codes given below.

(a) 1 and 3 (b) 1, 3 and 4
(c) 2 and 4 (d) 2 and 3

Ans. (d)

Exp. Increase in Government Expenditure and Deficit financing are not responsible for poverty. An increase in Government spending directly increases demand for goods and services. This increase economic activities in the economy and ultimately leads to a reduction of poverty among people.

Deficit financing is another way of increasing the money supply in the market so it also helps in the reduction poverty.

Inflation and short savings are responsible for poverty as inflation increases the prices of food and services hence poor people have to spend more money to purchase the same amount of goods which ultimately increases poverty among people.

Short savings leads to short capital formation .This decrease the economic activities in the economy which leads to a poverty among people.

31 Consider the following statements.

(Class 4, Class-XI, New NCERT)

1. The global Multidimensional Poverty Index (MPI) 2018 noted that 271 million people moved out of poverty between 2005-06 and 2015-16 in India.
2. As per the UNDP, the percentage of people living below the poverty line in India as of 2011 is above 50%.

Which of the statements given above is/are correct?

(a) Only 1 (b) Only 2
(c) Both 1 and 2 (d) Neither 1 nor 2

Ans. (c)

Exp. Both the statements (1) and (2) are correct. The global Multidimensional Poverty Index 2018 released by the United Nations noted that 271 million people moved out of poverty between 2015-16 in India.

The poverty rate in the country has nearly, falling from 55% to 28% over 10 year period. As per the United Nations Development Programme (UNDP), the percentage of people living below the poverty line in India as of 2011 is 53.4%. Still a big part of the population in India is living below the poverty line.

32 Multidimensional Poverty Index includes ....

(Chap 4, Class-XI, New NCERT)

1. Health 2. Education 3. Living standard

Select the correct answer from the codes given below.

(a) Only 1 (b) 2 and 3 (c) 1 and 2 (d) 1, 2 and 3

Ans. (d)

Exp. All of the above given dimensions are included in the multidimensional poverty index.

The Multidimensional Poverty Index (MPI) is published by the UNDP's Human Development Report Office and tracks deprivation across three dimensions and 10 indicators: health (child mortality, nutrition), education (years of schooling, enrollment) and living standards (water, sanitation, electricity, cooking fuel, floor, assets).

33 Consider the following Assertion (A) and Reason (R) and choose the correct code.

(Chap 3, Class-IX, New NCERT)

Assertion (A) There is a strong link between economic growth and poverty reduction.

Reason (R) Economic growth widens opportunities and provides the resources needed to invest in human development.

Codes

(a) Both A and R are true and R is the correct explanation of A.
(b) Both A and R are true, but R is not the correct explanation of A.
(c) A is true, but R is false.
(d) A is false, but R is true.

Ans. (a)

Exp. Both Assertion (A) and Reason (R) are true and Reason (R) is the correct explanation of Assertion (A).

There is a strong link between economic growth and poverty reduction. As we see in case of India, official poverty estimates were 45% in 1950 and it remained the same even in the early eighties. Since, eighties India's economic growth has been one of the fastest in the world. The higher growth rate helped significantly in the reduction of poverty.

Economic growth widens opportunities and provides the resources needed to invest in human development. This also encourages people to send their children including the girl child to schools in the hope of getting better economic returns from investing in education.

34 Consider the following Assertion (A) and Reason (R) and choose the correct code. *(Chap 2, Class-IX & X, Old NCERT)*

Assertion (A) India's poverty is primarily dependent on the fact that it is not possible for it to provide a profitable employment to its very large workforce.

Reason (R) Due to being less developed, India does not have enough land and capital to meet this huge population.

Codes

(a) Both A and R are true and R is the correct explanation of A.
(b) Both A and R are true, but R is not the correct explanation of A.
(c) A is true, but R is false.
(d) A is false, but R is true.

Ans. (a)

Exp. Both Assertion (A) and Reason (R) are true and Reason (R) is the correct explanation of Assertion (A).

India's poverty is primarily dependent on the fact that it is not possible to provide a profitable employment to its very large workforce.

For instance, more than half of the workers in the country are working in primary sector and are underemployed. India being a developing country, its does not have enough land and capital to meet huge population. In India, around 17% of world's population resides in only 2.4% of total geographical area of the world.

35 Identify the incorrect statements about Antyodaya Anna Yojana. *(Chap 4, Class-IX, New NCERT)*

(a) Antyodaya Anna Yojana (AAY) was launched in December 2000.
(b) Under this scheme, one crore of the poorest among the BPL families covered under the Targeted Public Distribution System were identified.
(c) 45 kilograms of foodgrains were made available to each eligible family at a highly subsidised rate of 2 per kg for rice and 3 per kg for wheat.
(d) Poor families were identified by the respective state rural development departments through a Below Poverty Line (BPL) Survey.

Ans. (c)

Exp. Statement (c) is incorrect about Antyodaya Anna Yojana as under Antyodaya Anna Yojana (AAY), 35 kg of foodgrains were made available to each eligible family at a highly subsidised rate of ₹ 3 per kg for rice and ₹ 2 per kg for wheat.

This scheme was launched in 2000 and under this scheme, one crore of the poorest among the BPL families were identified by the respective state rural development departments through a BPL Survey.

As of June 2023, 8.95 crore Antyodaya Anna Yojana (AAY) are getting benefits of Public Distribution System in the country through 5.45 lakh Fair Price Shops (FPSs) in India.

Families earning up to INR 15,000 annually can benefit from Antyodaya Anna Yojana.

36 Which of the following pairs is/are correctly matched? *(Chap 3, Class-IX, New NCERT)*

(a) IRDP – Subsidy and bank credit
(b) JRY – Economic infrastructure
(c) NOAPS – Pension
(d) All of the above

Ans. (d)

Exp. All of the given pairs are correctly matched.

Integrated Rural Development Programme (IRDP) was introduced in 1978-79 and universalised from 2nd October, 1980, aimed at providing assistance to the rural poor in the form of subsidy and bank credit for productive employment opportunities through successive plan periods.

The Jawahar Rozgar Yojana (JRY) was meant to generate meaningful employment opportunities for the unemployed and underemployed in rural areas through the creation of economic infrastructure and community and social assets.

National Old Age Pension Scheme (NOAPS) is given by the Central Government. The amount of old age pension is ₹ 200 per month for applicants aged 60-79. For applicants aged above 80 years, the amount has been revised to ₹ 500 a month.

37 Consider the following statements about the National Food Security Act, 2013. *(Chap 4, Class-IX, New NCERT)*

1. This Act provides for food and nutritional security at affordable prices and enable people to live a life with dignity.
2. Under this Act, 60% of the rural population and 50% of the urban population have been categorised as eligible households for food security.

Which of the statement(s) given above is/are incorrect?

(a) Only 1 (b) Only 2
(c) Both 1 and 2 (d) Neither 1 nor 2

Ans. (b)

Exp. Only statement (2) is incorrect about the National Food Security Act, 2013 as under this Act, 75% of the rural population and 50% of urban population have been categorised as eligible households for food security.

38 **Which of the following statements is incorrect regarding the Public Distribution System (PDS)?**

(Chap 4, Class-IX, New NCERT)

(a) From the very beginning, the coverage of PDS included the poor families only.

(b) In 1992, Revamped Public Distribution System (RPDS) was introduced in 1,700 blocks in the country with a target to provide the benefits of PDS to remote and backward areas.

(c) From June 1997, in a renewed attempt, Targeted Public Distribution System (TPDS) was introduced to adopt the principle of targeting the 'poor in all areas'.

(d) In 2000, Antyodaya Anna Yojana (AAY) and Annapurna Scheme (APS) were launched with special target groups of 'poorest of the poor' and 'indigent senior citizens', respectively.

Ans. (a)

Exp. Statement (a) is incorrect regarding Public Distribution System (PDS). In the beginning, the coverage of PDS was universal with no discrimination between poor and non-poor. Over the years, the policy related to PDS has been revised to make it more efficient and target based.

The PDS has proved to be the most effective instrument of government policy over the years in stabilising prices and making food available to consumers at affordable prices. It has been instrumental in averting widespread hunger and famine by supplying food from surplus regions of the country to the deficit ones.

39 **Which of the following statements is/are incorrect?**

(Chap 7, Class-XI, New NCERT)

1. **Open Unemployment** It refers to an unemployment that occurs at certain seasons of the years. The period of such unemployment varies from state to state, depending upon the methods of farming, the condition of soil, the type and numbers of crops grown, etc.
2. **Frictional Unemployment** It refers to temporary unemployment that exists during the period, wherein workers leave one job and join some other.
3. **Cyclical Unemployment** It is associated with the downswing and depression phases 9 business cycle. It is the most common type of unemployment in the developed capitalist economies.

Select the correct answer using the codes given below.

(a) Only 1
(b) Only 2
(c) Only 3
(d) 2 and 1

Ans. (a)

Exp. Only statement (1) is incorrect as Open unemployment is a situation when the people who are skilled and educated are unable to find a job that can fetch them regular income to sustain them. It occurs when the workforce increases at a much faster rate as compared to the number of opportunities in the country.
Example When an educated and skilled person is unable to find a job to earn a regular income.

Unemployment

40 **Consider the following statements.**

(Chap 7, Class-XI, New NCERT)

1. Cyclical unemployment figures in India are negligible.
2. The frictional unemployment also called as search unemployment.
3. Vulnerable employment rarely found in India.

Which of the statements given above is/are incorrect?

(a) 1 and 2 (b) Only 3
(c) 2 and 3 (d) 1 and 3

Ans. (b)

Exp. Only statement (3) is incorrect. Vulnerable employment means, people working informally, without proper job contracts and thus lack any legal protection. These persons are deemed unemployed since records of their work are never maintained. It is one of the main types of unemployment in India.

41 **Consider the following statements.**

(Chap 2, Class-IX, New NCERT)

1. Unemployment is said to exist when people who are willing to work at the going wages cannot find jobs.
2. The workforce population in India includes people from 18 years to 59 years.

Which of the statement(s) given above is/are correct?

(a) Only 1 (b) Only 2
(c) Both 1 and 2 (d) Neither 1 nor 2

Ans. (a)

Exp. Only statement (1) is correct. Unemployment is said to exist when people who are willing to work at the going wages cannot find jobs.

The National Statistical Office (previously known as CSO) defines unemployment as a situation in which all those who, owing to lack of work, are not working but either seek work through employment exchanges, intermediaries, friends or relatives or by making applications to prospective employers or express their willingness for availability of work under the prevailing condition of work and remunerations.

Statement (2) is incorrect because the workforce population includes people from 15 years to 59 years. Thus, the persons falling between these age group are called as workforce population.

42 Consider the following statements. *(Chap 7, Class-XI, New NCERT)*

1. The worker-population ratio is higher in rural areas as compared to urban areas.
2. Availability of Limited resources is one of the reasons of high worker population ratio in rural areas.

Which of the statements given above is/are correct?

(a) Only 1
(b) Only 2
(c) Both 1 and 2
(d) Neither 1 nor 2

Ans. (c)

Exp. Both the statements (1) and (2) are correct as people in rural areas have limited resources to earn a higher income and participate more in the employment market. Many do not go to schools, colleges and other training institutions.

Even if some go, they discontinue in the middle to join the workforce. Urban people have a variety of employment opportunities. They look for the appropriate job to suit their qualifications and skills. In rural areas, people cannot stay at home as their economic condition may not allow them to do so. Therefore, the worker-population ratio is higher in rural areas as compared to urban areas.

43 Which of the following statements is incorrect about unemployment? *(Chap 2, Class-IX, New NCERT)*

(a) Seasonal unemployment happens when people are not able to find jobs during some months of the year.
(b) In case of disguised unemployment people appear to be employed but their marginal output is zero.
(c) In educated unemployment many youth with matriculation, graduation and post-graduation degrees are not able to find jobs.
(d) Urban areas mostly have seasonal and disguised unemployment.

Ans. (d)

Exp. Statement (d) is incorrect about unemployment because in urban areas, seasonal and disguised unemployment is not seen mostly while educated unemployment has become common phenomenon. In these areas, many youth with matriculation, graduation and post-graduation degrees are not able to find the job. In urban areas, there is unemployment among technically qualified person on one hand, while there is a dearth of technical skills required for economic growth. Seasonal and disguised unemployment is mostly prevalent in rural areas.

44 Consider the following Assertion (A) and Reason (R) and choose the correct code. *(Chap 2, Class-IX, New NCERT)*

Assertion (A) If people cannot be used as a resource they naturally appear as a liability to the economy.

Reason (R) Unemployment has a detrimental impact on the overall growth of an economy.

Codes

(a) Both A and R are true and R is the correct explanation of A.
(b) Both A and R are true, but R is not the correct explanation of A.
(c) A is true, but R is false.
(d) A is false, but R is true.

Ans. (a)

Exp. Both Assertion (A) and Reason (R) are true and Reason (R) is the correct explanation of Assertion (A). If people cannot be used as a resource, they naturally appear as a liability to the economy. It wastes the resources, which could have been gainfully employed. Unemployment has a detrimental impact on the overall growth of an economy. It tends to increase economic overload. The dependence of the unemployed people on the working population increases.

45 Consider the following statements. *(Chap 7, Class-XI, New NCERT)*

Statement-I The kind of unemployment prevailing in Indian agricultural sector is disguised unemployment.

Statement-II Seasonal unemployment is virtually non existence in India.

Which one of the following is correct in respect of the above statements?

(a) Both Statement-I and Statement-II are correct and Statement-II is the correct explanation for Statement-I.
(b) Both Statement-I and Statement-II are correct and Statement-II is not the correct explanation for statement-I.
(c) Statement-I is correct but Statement-II is incorrect.
(d) Statement-I is incorrect but Statement-II is correct.

Ans. (c)

Exp. Statement-I is correct but Statement-II is incorrect. The type of unemployment in the agricultural sector of India where more people are employed than required is known as disguised unemployment. Disguised unemployment will occur when more people are engaged in a job than required. It is common form of unemployment in rural areas. However, Seasonal unemployment occurs during certain seasons of the year. Agricultural labourers in India rarely have work throughout the year.

46 Consider the following statements about worker population ratio. *(Chap 7, Class-XI, New NCERT)*

1. If the ratio is medium or low, it means that the engagement of people is greater.
2. If the ratio for a country is higher, it means that a very high proportion of its population is not involved directly in economic activities.

Which of the statements given above is/are correct?

(a) Only 1 (b) Only 2
(c) Both 1 and 2 (d) Neither 1 nor 2

Ans. (d)

Exp. Neither statement (1) nor (2) is correct about worker population ratio.

Worker population ratio is an indicator which is used for analysing the employment situation in the country. If the ratio for a country is medium or low, it means that a very high proportion of its population is not involved directly in economic activities.

If the ratio is higher, it means that the engagement of people is greater in economic activities. This ratio is also useful in knowing the proportion of population that is actively contributing to the production of goods and services of a country.

47 Which of the following statements is incorrect regarding types of employees? *(Chap 7, Class-XI, New NCERT)*

(a) Workers who own and operate an enterprise to earn their livelihood are known as self-employed.
(b) Casual workers are engaged in others' farms and in return, get remuneration for the work done.
(c) When a worker is engaged by someone or an enterprise and paid his or her wages on a regular basis, they are known as contractual employees.
(d) None of the above

***Ans.* (c)**

Exp. Statement (c) is incorrect regarding types of employees. When a worker is engaged by someone or an enterprise and paid his or her wages on a regular basis, they are known as 'regular salaried employees'. In regular salaries employment, both women and men are found to be engaged in greater proportion. According to International Labour Organisation, India had 23.99% salaried employees in the year 2020.

48 Consider the following statements. *(Chap 7, Class-XI, New NCERT)*

1. The process of moving from casual wage workforce to self-employment and regular salaried employment is known as casualisation of the workforce.
2. Casualisation of the workforce protects workers from vulnerability.

Which of the statements given above is/are correct?

(a) Only 1 (b) Only 2
(c) Both 1 and 2 (d) Neither 1 nor 2

***Ans.* (d)**

Exp. Neither statement (1) nor (2) is correct.

The process of moving from casual wage workforce to self-employment and regular salaried employment is not called casualisation of the workforce.

Casualisation of workforce is the process of moving from self-employment and regular salaried employment to casual wage work. Casualisation of the workforce makes the workers highly vulnerable as they are not paid on a regular basis.

49 In any poverty reduction strategy there is need to incorporate both self-employment and wage employment because *(Chap 7, Class-XI, New NCERT)*

1. self-employment is a major form of employment in rural area, wage employment.
2. dependence on wage employment will lead to total dependence on the employer.
3. otherwise it will increase the gap between the rich and the poor.
4. it will strengthen the asset base of the rich.

Select the correct answer using the codes given below.

(a) 1 and 2 (b) 3 and 4
(c) 1, 2 and 3 (d) 1, 2, 3 and 4

***Ans.* (d)**

Exp. All of the above statements are correct as with less growth or no presence of industries the major source of employment is agriculture or self-employment in rural areas.

The dependence on wage employment leads to total dependence on the employer. In such a situation, there is the exploitation the workers engaged in such activities.

Due to more employment opportunities in industries, the wage employable workers number will increase.

It will create more purchasing power among the workers and ultimately the demand for goods will increase which will increase the asset base of the rich people as people tend to increase the production of goods due to increase in demand. This ultimately increases, the gap between rich and poor.

50 With reference to 'employment in formal sector', which of the following statement(s) is/are correct? *(Chap 7, Class-XI, New NCERT)*

1. Information relating to employment in the formal sector is collected by the Ministry of Personnel.
2. All the public sector establishments and those private sector establishments, which employ 10 hired workers or more are called formal sector establishments.

Select the correct answer using the codes given below.

(a) Only 1 (b) Only 2
(c) Both 1 and 2 (d) Neither 1 nor 2

***Ans.* (b)**

Exp. Statement (2) is correct with reference to 'employment in formal sector'. The criterion of 10 workers is utilised for classification of establishments into formal or informal sector. It includes both public sector as well as private sector establishments.

Statement (1) is incorrect as the information relating to employment in the formal sector is collected by the Union Ministry of Labour through employment exchanges located in different parts of the country.

51 **Which of the following offices and their sources of data on unemployment is incorrectly matched?**
(Chap 2, Class-X, New NCERT)

(a) Registrar General - Reports of Census of India
(b) National Statistical Office - Reports of Employment and Unemployment Situation
(c) Central Statistical Organisation - Annual Periodic Labour Force Survey
(d) Directorate General of Employment - Registration with Employment Exchanges

Ans. (c)

Exp. Pair (c) is incorrectly matched. Annual Periodic Labour Force Survey was launched by National Sample Survey Office (NSSO) in April, 2017. It estimate the key employment and unemployment indicators. Whereas other pairs are correctly matched.

52 **Consider the following statements.**
(Chap 4, Class-IX, New NCERT)

1. Start Up India Scheme promotes entrepreneurship of SCs or STs across the country.
2. Stand Up India Scheme aims to facilitate bank loan at least one women borrower per bank branch.

Which of the statement (s) given above is/are incorrect?

(a) Only 1 (b) Only 2
(c) Both 1 and 2 (d) Neither 1 nor 2

Ans. (a)

Exp. Statement (1) is incorrect. Start Up India Scheme was launched in 2016 and aims at developing an ecosystem that promotes and nurtures entrepreneurship across the country. It was launched in 2016.

53 **Consider the following statements.**
(Chap 4, Class-IX, New NCERT)

1. The NULM focuses on organising Urban poor in Self Help Groups.
2. Pradhan Mantri Kaushal Vikas Yojana focuses on labour market.
3. Pradhan Mantri Jan Dhan Yojana focuses on unbanked poor.

Which of the statement(s) given above is/are correct?

(a) 1 and 2 (b) 1, 2 and 3 (c) 2 and 3 (d) 1 and 3

Ans. (b)

Exp. All the given statements (1), (2) and (3) are correct. The National Urban Livelihood Mission (NULM) focuses on organising urban poor in Self Help Groups, creating opportunities for skill development leading to market-based employment and helping them to set up self-employment ventures by ensuring easy access to credit.

Pradhan Mantri Kaushal Vikas Yojana will focus on fresh entrants to the labour market, especially labour market and class X and XII dropouts.

Pradhan Mantri Jan Dhan Yojana aimed at direct benefit transfer of subsidy, pension, insurance etc. The scheme particularly targets the unbanked poor.

54 **Match the following.** *(Chap 4, Class-IX, New NCERT)*

	Name of Programme		Year of Starting
A.	Atmanirbhar Bharat	1.	May, 2020
B.	Pradhan Mantri Garib Kalyan Anna Yojana	2.	March, 2020
C.	Atal Pension Yojana	3.	May, 2015
D.	Pradhan Mantri Jan Dhan Yojana	4.	August, 2014

Codes

	A	B	C	D
(a)	1	2	3	4
(b)	2	3	4	1
(c)	3	4	2	1
(d)	4	3	1	2

Ans. (a)

Exp. The correct matching is A-1, B-2, C-3, D-4.
Government of India on 12th May, 2020 announced an economic stimulus package for 20 lakh crore (estimated at 10% of the GDP) towards building an Atmanirbhar Bharat or a self reliant, resilient India.

Pradhan Mantri Garib Kalyan Yojana is a part of Pradhan Mantri Garib Kalyan package launched on 26th March, 2020 to help the poor fight the battle against COVID-19.
Atal Pension Yojana was launched in May, 2015 to create a universal social security system for all Indians.

Pradhan Mantri Jan Dhan Yojana was launched 28th August, 2014. It aims to provide access to various financial services.

Chapter 05

Rural and Urban Development and Basic Infrastructure

Rural and Urban Development and Basic Infrastructure

Rural Development

Introduction

- An action plan for the economic and social upliftment of rural areas; Main objectives are
  - To improve productivity and wages of people
  - To demolish unemployment
  - To provide the basic and elementary needs

Ministry of Rural Development

- Established under Agriculture and Food Ministry
- Formed on 20th January, 1980
- A branch of the Government of India

Issues in Rural Development

Rural Credit

- Growth depends on infusion of capital, non-agriculture sectors
- **Types of Rural Credit**
  - **Short term** Period of less than 15 months
  - **Medium term** Period range 15 months to 5 years
  - **Long term** More than 5 years

Rural Marketing

- Lack of storage facilities
- Absence of market information

Rural Development Schemes

Pradhan Mantri Aawas Yojana (Gramin)

- Launched to achieve housing for all by 2022
- To help rural people below the BPL

Survey of Villages and Mapping with Improvised Technology in Village Areas (SVAMITVA)

- Launched on 24th April, 2021 ; Aim to provide rural people with the right to document their properties

Shyama Prasad Mukherjee Rurban Mission (SPMRM)

- Launched on 21st February, 2016
- To providing Urban Amenities

Sansad Aadarsh Gram Yojana (SAGY)

- Launched in 2014
- Scheme called MP to make one GP of their choice

Deen Dayal Antyodaya Yojana (DAY-NRLM)

- Launched by ministry of rural development in June 2011
- Involves working with community institution

Urban Development

Urban Areas

- Recognised as engines of inclusive economic growth
- Minimum population of 5000 persons; Density of population of atleast 400 persons per squaremeter

Urban Development Schemes

- PM Vishwakarma Yojana
  - PM Vishwakarma was launched on 17th September, 2023 by PM Narendra Modi to provide end to end support to artisans and craftspeople, who work their hands and tools
- **PM-PRANAM**
  - PM Programme for Restoration, Awareness, Nourishment and Amelioration of Mother Earth - (PM-PRANAM) was launched in Union Budget 2023-24 to promote. The balance use of chemical and alternative fertilisers, generative agriculture (RA)
- **Mahila Samman Saving Scheme**
  - To ensure the financial growth of women, Government of India launched the Mahila Samman Saving Certificate Scheme on April 2013
- **Viksit Bharat @ 2047**
  - Vocie of youth was launched on 11th December, 2013 to empowering youth of the nation
- **Lakhpati Didi Scheme**
  - Lakhpati Didi Scheme launced on 23rd December, 2023 to provide training in various skills such as plumbing, tailoring and weaving, which would enable them to earn a sustainable income of at least 1 lakh per annum
- **Rooftop Solarisation Scheme**
  - Prime Minister Narendra Modi had launched the Rooftop Solarisation on 13th February, 2024
  - This scheme provides central financial assistance of 30,000 subsidy for 1 kw system
  - The programme's goal is to increase rooftop solar installed capacity to 40 GW by March 2026

SOURCE *New NCERT Class XI (Rural Development), New NCERT Class XI (Infrastructure)*

1 **Which of the following is/are included in non-agricultural production activities?**

(Chap 6, Class-XI, New NCERT)

1. Health Facilities
2. Education
3. Dairy
4. Food Processing
5. Small-scale manufacturing
6. Transportation

Codes

(a) 2 and 3 (b) 4, 5 and 6
(c) 1, 2, 5 and 6 (d) 1, 2, 3, 4, 5 and 6

Ans. (d)

Exp. All of the above given conditions that is health facilities, education, dairy, food processing, small-scale manufacturing and transportation are included in non-agricultural production activities. Non-farm agricultural activities are such activities which do not involve agriculture and are important for rural development.

The non-farm activities help in establishing market in the village, act as a source of income for the farmers and also provide employment to landless labourers.

2 **Consider the following statements with respect to the significance of rural development.**

(Chap 6, Class-XI, New NCERT)

1. More than two-third of India's population depends on agriculture that is yet to become productive enough.
2. One-third of rural India still lives in poverty.

Which of the statements given above is/are incorrect?

(a) Only 1 (b) Only 2
(c) Both 1 and 2 (d) Neither 1 nor 2

Ans. (b)

Exp. Only statement (2) is incorrect with respect to the significance of rural development because one-fourth (not one-third) of rural India still lives in poverty.

The majority of poor live in rural areas do not have access to the basic necessities of life that is the reason we need a developed rural India, if our nation want to achieve a real progress.

3 **Which of the following areas are lagging behind in the overall development of the village economy?**

(Chap 6, Class-XI, New NCERT)

1. Land reforms
2. Infrastructure development like electricity, irrigation
3. Literacy
4. Health infrastructure

Codes

(a) 1, 2 and 4 (b) 2 and 4
(c) 3 and 4 (d) 1, 2, 3 and 4

Ans. (d)

Exp. All the areas given in the options are lagging behind in the overall development of the village economy. Rural development is a comprehensive term and focusses on action for development of areas that are lagging behind in the overall development of the village economy.

Some of the areas which are challenging and need new initiatives for development in rural areas are

- Land reforms like size, acquisition and distribution of agricultural land.
- Infrastructure development like electricity, irrigation, credit, marketing, transport facilities including construction of village roads to nearby highways, facilities for agriculture research and extension and information dissemination.
- Development of human resources including literacy (more specifically female literacy), skill development, health, sanitation and public health.

4 **Consider the following Assertion (A) and Reason (R) and choose the correct code.**

(Chap 6, Class-XI, New NCERT)

Assertion (A) Growth of rural economy depends primarily on infusion of capital, from time to time, to realise higher productivity in agricultural and non-agricultural sectors.

Reason (R) As the time of gestation between crop sowing and realisation of income after production is quite long, farmers borrow from various sources to meet their initial investment on seeds and fertilisers.

Codes

(a) Both A and R are true and R is the correct explanation of A.
(b) Both A and R are true, but R is not the correct explanation of A.
(c) A is true, but R is false.
(d) A is false, but R is true.

Ans. (a)

Exp. Both Assertion (A) and Reason (R) are true and Reason (R) is the correct explanation of Assertion (A). Growth of rural economy depends primarily on infusion of capital, from time to time, to realise higher productivity in agriculture and non-agriculture sectors.

It is to be noted that the time of gestation between crop sowing and realisation of income after production is quite long. As a result, farmers borrow from various sources to meet their initial investment on seeds, fertilisers etc. That's why there is a need of capital from time to time for the growth of rural economy.

5 **Consider the following statements.**

(Chap 6, Class-XI, New NCERT)

1. The NABARD was set up in 1982 as an apex body to coordinate the activities of all institutions involved in the rural financing system.
2. The bank has been entrusted with matters concerning policy, planning and operation in the

field of credit for agriculture and other economic activities in rural areas in India.

3. The Green Revolution brought about major change in the credit system as it led to the diversification of the portfolio of rural credit towards production-orientation lending.

How many of the statements given above is/are correct?

(a) Only one (b) Only two
(c) All three (d) None of these

Ans. (c)

Exp. All three statements i.e. (1), (2) and (3) are correct as NABARD is India's apex development bank, established in 1982 under an Act of Parliament to promote sustainable and equitable agriculture and rural development.

It coordinates the rural financing activities of all institutions engaged in developmental work at the field level and maintains liaison with Government of India , State Governments, Reserve Bank of India (RBI) and other national level institutions concerned with policy formulation.

The Green Revolution was a harbinger of major changes in the credit system as it led to the diversification of the portfolio of rural credit towards production- oriented lending.

6 **Diversification of agriculture is expected to increase farmers income. Which of the following is/are diversification of agriculture?**

(Chap 5, Class-XI, New NCERT)

1. Change in cropping pattern
2. Mixed farming
3. Livestock rearing

Select the correct answer using the codes given below.

(a) Only 1 (b) 1 and 2
(c) 2 and 3 (d) All of these

Ans. (d)

Exp. All of these above given options refers to diversification of agriculture. Agriculture diversification refers to either a change in cropping pattern or the farmers opting for other non-farming options like poultry farming, animal husbandry, etc.

This practice allows farmers to expand the production, which helps generate a higher level of income. Following are the major advantages of crop diversification.

1. Increase in income of small farm holdings,
2. Less risk for price fluctuation,
3. Climatic variability,
4. Balancing food demand,
5. Increasing the production of quality fodder for livestock animals,
6. Beneficial for conserving natural resources, etc.

7 **Consider the following statements about Self-Help Groups.** *(Chap 6, Class-XI, New NCERT)*

1. The SHGs promote thrift in small proportions by a minimum contribution from each member.
2. From the pooled money, credit is given to the needy members to be repayable in small installments at reasonable interest rates.

Which of the statements given above is/are correct?

(a) Only 1 (b) Only 2
(c) Both 1 and 2 (d) Neither 1 nor 2

Ans. (c)

Exp. Both the statements (1) and (2) are correct about Self-Help Groups.

Self-Help Groups (SHGs) are informal associations of people who choose to come together to find ways for improving their living conditions. They play a prominent role in financial inclusion of rural India. They promote money pooling by small contribution by all the members to help any of the member who need help at any point of time. SHGs have emerged to fill the gap in the formal credit system.

8 **Consider the following statements.**

(Chap 5, Class-XI, Tamil Nadu Board) (IAS Pre 2023)

1. The Self-Help Group (SHG) programme was originally initiated by the State Bank of India by providing microcredit to the financially deprived.
2. In a SHG, all members of a group take responsibility for a loan that an individual member takes.
3. The Regional Rural Banks and Scheduled Commercial Banks support SHGs.

How many of the above statements is/are correct?

(a) Only one (b) Only two
(c) All three (d) None of these

Ans. (b)

Exp. Only two statements i.e., (2) and (3) are correct. In a SHGs, when a member of the SHG requires a loan, the group collectively evaluates the member's need and repayment capacity. If the loan is approved the individual member becomes the recipient of the funds. However, the entire group takes joint liability for the repayment of the loan.

Regional Rural Banks and Scheduled Commercial Banks supports SHGs by extending credit facilities to Micro-finance Insitutions (MFIs) which then on lend funds to SHGs and other microfinance clients.

Statement (1) is incorrect because the Self-Help Groups started in the late 1980s by the Non-Governmental Organisations (NGOs) and development agencies.

NABARD (The National Bank for Agriculture and Rural Development) played a significant role in the promotion and scaling up SHGs by providing financial support, capacity building initiatives and policy framework.

9 **Consider the following events and arrange them in chronological order.** *(Chap 6, Class-XI, New NCERT) (UPPSC Pre 2020)*

1. Establishment of NABARD
2. Self-Help Group Bank Linkage Programme
3. Kisan Credit Card Plan
4. Establishment of Regional Rural Bank

Codes

(a) 4, 1, 2, 3 (b) 4, 2, 3, 1 (c) 1, 2, 3, 4 (d) 4, 3, 2, 1

Ans. (a)

Exp. The correct chronological order of events is 4, 1, 2, 3.

Regional Rural Banks (RRBs) These were established in 1975 to dispense adequate credit at cheaper rates to rural population.

NABARD National Bank for Agriculture and Rural Development was set up in 1982 as an apex body to coordinate the activities of all institutions involved in the rural financing system.

Self-Help Group Bank Linkage Programme It was started in 1992 by the NABARD to link the unorganised sector with the formal banking sector.

Kisan Credit Card Plan It was introduced in 1998 by NABARD to provide term loans to farmers for their agricultural needs.

10 **Rural credit can be classified into the following categories.** *(Chap 6, Class-XI, New NCERT)*

1. Short term credit–for a period of less than 15 months.
2. Medium term credit–for a period of 3 years.
3. Long term credit–for a period of upto 5 years.

Which of the statements given above is/are correct?

(a) Only 1 (b) 1 and 2 (c) 2 and 3 (d) All of these

Ans. (a)

Exp. Only statement (1) is correct with respect to the rural credit categories. The Indian farmers require credit to meet their short term needs viz, purchasing seeds, fertilisers, paying wages to hired workers etc. for a period of less than 15 months.

Statements (2) and (3) are incorrect because medium term credit is a type of credit that includes credit requirements of farmers for a medium period ranging between 15 months to 5 years. Period of long term credit is more than 5 years. The purpose of long term credit is buying additional land, horticulture etc.

11 **Consider the following statements about infrastructure.** *(Chap 8, Class-XI, New NCERT)*

1. Infrastructure provides supporting services in the main areas of industrial and agricultural production, domestic and foreign trade and commerce.
2. It includes roads, railways, ports, airports, dams, power stations, oil and gas pipelines, tele-communication facilities, etc.

Which of the statements given above is/are correct?

(a) Only 1
(b) Only 2
(c) Both 1 and 2
(d) Neither 1 nor 2

Ans. (c)

Exp. Both the statements (1) and (2) are correct about infrastructure. Infrastructure is the support system, which depends on the efficient working of a modern industrial economy. It provides supporting services in the main areas of industrial and agricultural production, domestic and foreign trade and commerce.

Infrastructural services include roads, railways, ports, airports, dams, power stations, oil and gas pipelines, telecommunication facilities etc. Some of these facilities have a direct impact on production of goods and services while other give indirect support by building the social sector of economy.

12 **Consider the following statements about organic farming.** *(Chap 5, Class-XI, New NCERT)*

Statement-I Organic farming is based on the usage of organic fertilisers.

Statement-II This method of farming is used to create toxin-free food for consumers while also maintaining soil-fertility and contributing to ecological balance.

Which one of the following is correct in respect of the above statements?

(a) Both Statement-I and Statement-II are correct and Statement-II is the correct explanation for Statement-I.
(b) Both Statement-I and Statement-II are correct and Statement-II is not the correct explanation for Statement-I.
(c) Statement-I is correct but Statement-II is incorrect.
(d) Statement-I is incorrect but Statement-II is correct.

Ans. (a)

Exp. Both Statement-I and Statement-II are correct and Statement-II is the correct explanation for Statement-I.

Organic farming, also known as ecological farming or biological farming, is an agricultural system that uses fertilisers of organic origin such as compost manure, green manure and bone meal and places emphasis on techniques such as crop rotation and companion planting. Organic farming uses fewer pesticides, reduces soil erosion, decreases nitrate leaching into groundwater and surface water and recycles animal wastes back into the farm.

13 **Consider the following statements.** *(Chap 8, Class-XI, New NCERT)*

1. HRIDAY was launched in 2015 with the aim of bringing together urban planning, economic growth and heritage conservation in an inclusive manner.

2. NULM was launched by the Ministry of Housing and Urban Poverty Alleviation, Government of India.

Which of the statements given above is/are correct?

(a) Only 1
(b) Only 2
(c) Both 1 and 2
(d) Neither 1 nor 2

Ans. (c)

Exp. Both the statements (1) and (2) are correct.

The National Heritage City Development and Augmentation Yojana (HRIDAY), a central sector scheme of the Government of India.

It was launched on 21st January, 2015 with an aim of bringing together urban planning, economic growth and heritage conservation in an inclusive manner and with objective of preserving the heritage character of the city.

National Urban Livelihoods Mission (NULM) was launched by the Ministry of Housing and Urban Poverty Alleviation (MHUPA), Government of India on 23rd September, 2013 by replacing the existing Swarna Jayanti Shahari Rozgar Yojana.

14 Consider the following statements in relation to Janani Suraksha Yojana. *(Chap 5, Class-XI, New NCERT) (IAS Pre 2023)*

1. It is a safe motherhood intervention of the State Health Departments.
2. Its objective is to reduce maternal and neonatal mortality among poor pregnant women.
3. It aims to promote institutional delivery among poor pregnant women.
4. Its objective includes providing public health facilities to sick infants up to one year of age.

How many of the statements given above is/are correct?

(a) Only one (b) Only two (c) Only three (d) All four

Ans. (b)

Exp. Only two statements i.e., (2) and (3) are correct as Janani Suraksha Yojana (JSY) is being implemented with the objective of reducing maternal and neonatal mortality by promoting institutional delivery among poor pregnant women.

Statements (1) and (4) are incorrect because Janani Suraksha Yojana is a safe motherhood intervention under the National Rural Health Mission (NRHM). It is a 100% centrally sponsored scheme.

JSY provides cash assistance to pregnant women to cover the costs of delivery and postpartum care. The amount of cash assistance varies depending on the type of facility where the woman delivers and the state in which she resides.

Under the Janani Shishu Suraksha Karyakaram scheme (and not under JSY), all pregnant women and infants will get free treatment benefits at public health institutions including zero expenses delivery.

15 Consider the following statements in the context of interventions being undertaken under Anaemia Mukt Bharat Strategy.

(Chap 5, Class-XI, New NCERT) (IAS Pre 2023)

1. It provides prophylactic calcium supplementation for pre-school children, adolescents and pregnant women.
2. It runs a campaign for delayed cord clamping at the time of child birth.
3. It provides for periodic deworming to children and adolescents.
4. It addresses non-nutritional causes of anaemia in endemic pockets with special focus on malaria, hemoglobinopathies and fluorosis.

How many of the statements given above is/are correct?

(a) Only one
(b) Only two
(c) Only three
(d) All four

Ans. (c)

Exp. Only three statements (2), (3) and (4) are correct. The Anaemia Mukt Bharat Strategy runs a campaign for delayed cord clamping at the time of child birth. It provides for periodic deworming to children and adolescents. It addresses non-nutritional causes of anaemia in endemic pockets with special focus on malaria, hemoglobinopathies and fluorosis.

It focuses on six target beneficiary groups, through six interventions and six institutional mechanisms to achieve the envisaged target under the POSHAN Abhiyan.

16 'Mission Indradhanush' launched by the Government of India pertains to

(Chap 5, Class-XI, New NCERT) (IAS Pre 2016)

(a) immunisation of children and pregnant women.
(b) construction of smart cities across the country.
(c) India's own search for the Earth like planets in outer space.
(d) new educational policy.

Ans. (a)

Exp. 'Mission Indradhanush' launched by the Government of India pertains to immunisation of children and pregnant women. Mission Indradhanush is a health mission of the Government of India.

The scheme seeks to drive towards 90% full immunisation coverage of India and sustain the same by the year of 2022.

Mission Indradhanush is a government- sponsored programme launched in 2014 with the objective of achieving full immunisation coverage for children under the age of two years.

The percentage of children under the age of two years who have received all recommended vaccines has increased from 62% in 2014 to 83% in 2023.

Chapter 06

Agriculture

Agriculture

Basics of Indian Agriculture

Introduction
- Play important role in Indian economy
- Come under the Primary Sector
- Contribute 19.9% to the total GDP

Reforms in Indian Agriculture
- In 1951, First attempt made to bring change
- Policies of land reform and Green revolution was made to replace the problem

Significance of Agriculture in Indian Economy
- Contribution of Agriculture in National Income is about 19.9% in 2021-22
- Contribution of Agriculture in Employment is about 52% people depend on it
- Contribution in Economic Growth and Capital Formation, increase overall GDP

Agriculture Marketing
- Include operations such as collecting, grading, processing, preserving and financing

Various Marketing Methods
- Rural Primary Method
- Cooperative marketing
- Contract farming
- Commodity market; Future market

Organic Farming
- System of farm design and management create ecosystem in agriculture

Government Initiatives in the field of Organic farming
- One District-One Product
- PM Formalisation of Micro food Processing Enterprises; Zero Budget Natural Farming

Minimum Support Price, Food Security and Agriculture Allied Sector

Minimum Support Price (MSP)
- Rate at which Government purchases crops from farmers
- Government steps for MSP
  - Pradhan Mantri Annadata Aay Sanrakshan Abhiyan
  - Pradhan Mantri Kisan Samman Nidhi

Food Security
- All people all time access sufficient safe and nutritious food to meet the food preferences
- **Elements** Food availability, Food accessibility, Food affordability
- **Schemes** National food Security Mission (2007), Public distribution system (PDS), National food security Act 2013

Agriculture Allied Sector
- Livestock /Animal Rearing
- Fisheries Sector
- Horticulture
- Floriculture

Government steps related to Agriculture allied section
- Horticulture Cluster Development Programme
- Kisan Sarathi
- Agriculture Infrastructure Fund
- Biotech Kisan Programme
- Aroma Mission and Floriculture Mission
- National Gene Bank

Agriculture Institution
- Indian Council for Agriculture Research
- Food and Agriculture Organisation

Agriculture in Five Years Plans and Agriculture Revolutions

- **First (1951-1956)** The agriculture sector was given priority; Work on projects like Bhakra Nangal Dam, Hirakud Dam
- **Second (1956-61)** A total of 20% revenue was allocated to agriculture sector
- **Third (1961-66)** Effect of Green Revolution start Giving Positive results; Agriculture was again back in focus
- **Fourth (1969-74)** Special emphasis was laid to plan research in agriculture
- **Fifth (1974-79)** 15% revenue was allotted for agriculture sector; Results achieve more than that
- **Sixth (1980-85)** Entire focus of this plan was on population control and modernisation
- **Seventh (1985-90)** Other crops exceeded the setted target; Modernisation in agriculture sector able to reduce poverty in rural areas
- **Eighth (1992-97)** Agriculture growth was 4.7%, LPG were the major focus
- **Ninth (1997-2002)** Agriculture sector grew at 2.06%
- **Tenth (2002-07)** National Agriculture policy was adopted; Special emphasis were given on soil
- **Eleventh (2007-12)** A target of 4% annual growth rate was set
- **Twelfth (2012-17)** 4% annual growth rate was set as target

SOURCE *New NCERT Class IX* (The Story of Village Palampur), *New NCERT Class IX* (Food Security of India), *New NCERT Class IX* (People as a Resource), *New NCERT Class XI* (Indian Economy 1950-1990), *New NCERT Class XI* (Rural Development)

1 Which of the following statements is incorrect regarding agriculture? *(Chap 1, Class-IX, New NCERT)*

(a) Growing more than one crop on a piece of land during the year is known as multiple cropping.
(b) Mono cropping is the most common way of increasing production on a given piece of land.
(c) During the rainy season, farmers grow jowar and bajra.
(d) In the winter season, fields are sown with wheat.

Ans. (b)

Exp. Statement (b) is incorrect regarding agriculture as multiple cropping (not mono cropping) is the most common way of increasing production on a given piece of land. To grow more than one crop on a piece of land during the year is called multiple cropping. On the other hand, mono cropping is the practice of growing the same crop on the same piece of land, year after year.

2 Consider the following statements about the condition of the agriculture sector after independence. *(Chap 4, Class-IX, New NCERT)*

1. The low productivity of the agricultural sector forced India to import food from the United States of America (USA).
2. Land ceiling fixed the minimum size of land which could be owned by an individual.

Which of the statements given above is/are correct?

(a) Only 1 (b) Only 2
(c) Both 1 and 2 (d) Neither 1 nor 2

Ans. (a)

Exp. Only statement (1) is correct about the condition of the agriculture sector after independence.

Due to lack of resources, primitive agriculture techniques, informal sources of credit and negligible public investment in agriculture, the total production is very low and insufficient to fulfill the needs of population. This low productivity of the agricultural sector forced India to import food from the United States of America.

Statement (2) is incorrect because land ceiling fixed the maximum (not the minimum) size of land which could be owned by the individual. Land ceiling was the policy to promote equity in the agricultural sector.

3 Consider the following statements regarding agriculture in India. *(Chap 2, Class-IX, New NCERT)*

1. Agriculture and allied sectors contribute more than 17% of Gross Domestic Product of India.
2. Share in total employment by agriculture as high as 49%.

Which of the statements given above is/are correct?

(a) Only 1
(b) Only 2
(c) Both 1 and 2
(d) Neither 1 nor 2

Ans. (c)

Exp. Both the statements (1) and (2) are correct regarding agriculture in India. Agriculture sector includes core farming, animal husbandry, dairy, etc. Agriculture is a dominant sector in India as it contributes 17% to the total Gross Domestic Product (GDP). Agriculture plays an important role in the Indian economy as around 49% of the population is still dependent on agriculture and allied activities.

4 Consider the following statements. *(Chap 2, Class-XI, New NCERT)*

1. Yield is measured as crop produced on a given piece of land during one year.
2. Till the mid-1960s, the seeds used in cultivation were traditional ones with relatively low yields.
3. HYV seeds needed plenty of water, chemical fertilisers and pesticides to produce the best results.

How many of the above statements is/are correct?

(a) Only one (b) Only two
(c) All three (d) None of these

Ans. (b)

Exp. Only two statements i.e., (2) and (3) are correct as till the mid-1960s, the seeds used in cultivation were traditional ones with relatively low yields.

HYV seeds, needed plenty of water, chemical fertilisers and pesticides to produce best results.

Statement (1) is incorrect because crop yield is a standard measurement of the amount of agricultural production harvested-yield of a crop-per unit of land area.

5 Consider the following statements. *(Chap 2, Class-IX, New NCERT)*

1. The Green Revolution in the late 1960s introduced the Indian farmer to cultivation of wheat and rice using HYV seeds.
2. HYV seeds needed plenty of water, chemical fertilisers and pesticides to produce best results.

Which of the statements given above is/are incorrect?

(a) Only 1
(b) Only 2
(c) Both 1 and 2
(d) Neither 1 nor 2

Ans. (d)

Exp. Neither statement (1) nor (2) is incorrect.

The Green Revolution in late 1960s introduced the Indian farmers to cultivation of wheat and rice using HYV seeds. In comparison to the traditional seeds, the HYV seeds promised to produce much greater amounts of grain on a single plant.

HYV seeds needed plenty of water, chemical fertilisers and pesticides to produce best results. Thus, higher yields were possible only from a combination of HYV seeds, better irrigation, chemical fertilisers, pesticides, etc.

6 With reference to Green Revolution in India, consider the following statements. *(Chap 2, Class-XI, New NCERT)*

1. In India, it was made successful by Norman Borlaug.
2. The achievements of Green Revolution were rise in cereal production especially wheat and rice, change in cropping pattern in favour of wheat and increase in employment opportunities.

Which of the statements given above is/are correct?

(a) Only 1 (b) Only 2
(c) Both 1 and 2 (d) Neither 1 nor 2

Ans. (b)

Exp. Only statement (2) given above is correct as the achievements of the Green Revolution were the rise in cereal production especially wheat and rice, a change in cropping pattern in favour of wheat, and an increase in employment opportunities.

Statement (1) is incorrect because in India it was made successful by Dr M S Swaminathan. In 1970 Norman E. Borlaug who was an agrononist from America was awarded the Nobel Peace Prize in 1970 for a lifetime of work to feed a hungry world. The term Green Revolution was coined by Dr William Gaud.

7 Which of the following statements is incorrect regarding the effects of the Green Revolution? *(Chap 1, Class-IX, New NCERT)*

(a) Scientific reports indicate that the Green Revolution has overused the natural resource base.
(b) In many areas, Green Revolution is associated with the loss of soil fertility due to increased use of chemical fertilisers.
(c) Continuous use of groundwater for tubewell irrigation has led to the depletion of the water-table.
(d) None of the above

Ans. (d)

Exp. None of the given above statements are incorrect regarding the effects of the Green Revolution.

It is necessary to use land carefully as it is a natural resource.

Scientific reports indicate that the modern farming methods have overused the natural resource base.

In many areas, Green Revolution resulted into loss of soil fertility due to increased use of chemical fertilisers. Chemical fertilisers can also kill bacteria and micro-organisms in soil and result into loss of soil fertility.

Continuous use of groundwater for tubewell irrigation has also led to the depletion of water-table.

Chemical fertilisers provide minerals which dissolve in water and immediately available to plants. But these may not be retained in soil for long and may escape from soil and pollute groundwater, rivers and lakes.

8 With reference to the use of chemical fertilisers in Indian agriculture, which of the given statement(s) is/are correct? *(Chap 1, Class-IX, New NCERT)*

1. Punjab is the largest consumer of chemical fertilisers in India.
2. A substantial amount of fertiliser subsidy also benefits the fertiliser industry.

Select the correct answer using the codes given below.

(a) Only 1 (b) Only 2
(c) Both 1 and 2 (d) Neither 1 nor 2

Ans. (c)

Exp. Both the statements (1) and (2) are correct regarding the use of chemical fertilisers in Indian agriculture.

The Green Revolution first initiated in Punjab encouraged farmers besides using HYV seeds to use chemical fertilisers on extensive scale. However, with declining productivity, farmers in Punjab were compelled to use more chemical fertilisers to sustain productivity of land, this has increased the cost of production.

In India, fertiliser subsidy is granted to fertiliser industry which in turn is responsible for passing it to farmers. However, due to discrepancies present in this mechanism, a substantial amount of fertiliser subsidy also benefits the fertiliser industry.

9 Consider the following statements. *(Chap 2, Class-XI, New NCERT)*

1. Agricultural growth has direct impact on poverty eradication.
2. Commercial crops are those crops which are produced for trade purpose and not for self consumption by the farmers.

Which of the statements given above is/are correct?

(a) Only 1 (b) Only 2
(c) Both 1 and 2 (d) Neither 1 nor 2

Ans. (c)

Exp. Both the statements (1) and (2) are correct as poverty reduction has been associated with growth in yields and in agricultural labour productivity. The sectoral pattern of growth changes systematically as countries develop, posing challenges for governments searching for the best balance of macroeconomic, social and sectoral policies to foster poverty reduction.

Commercial crops are those crops which are planted for the purpose of selling on the market or for export to make profit, as distinguished from subsistence crops planted for the purpose of self-supply of the farmer like livestock feeding or food for the family. Examples of typical food and non-food cash crops are cereals, oilseeds, coffee, cocoa, sugar cane, vegetables and fruits (e.g. avocado and oranges), peanuts, cotton and tobacco.

10 **Consider the following factors.**

(Chap 2, Class-XI, New NCERT)

1. Demand and Supply
2. Cost of Production
3. Price tends in the domestic and international market
4. Terms of trade between agricultural and non-agriculture sector

How many of the above-mentioned factors are taken into consideration for the determination of MSP by the Commission for Agricultural Costs and Prices (CACP)?

(a) Only one (b) Only two (c) Only three (d) All four

Ans. (d)

Exp. All the four above-mentioned factors are taken into consideration for the determination of MSP. Commission for Agricultural Costs and Prices (CACP) submits its recommendations to the government in the form of price policy reports every years. Separately for five groups of commodities namely kharif crops, rabi crops, sugarcane, raw jute and copra. While recommending the price policy of various commodities under its mandate, the commission takes into consideration.

- Demand and Supply
- Cc t of Production
- Price trends in the market, both domestic and international
- Intercrop price parity.
- A minimum of 50% as the margin over cost.
- Terms of trade between agricultural and non-agriculture sector.

11 **Consider the following statements.**

(Chap 4, Class-IX, New NCERT) (IAS Pre 2023)

1. The Government of India provides Minimum Support Price for Niger (Guizotia abyssinica) seeds.
2. Niger is cultivated as a kharif crop.
3. Some tribal people in India use niger seed oil for cooking.

How many of the above statements is/are correct?

(a) Only one
(b) Only two
(c) All three
(d) None of these

Ans. (c)

Exp. All three statements i.e., (1), (2) and (3) are correct as Niger seeds, scientifically known as Guizotia abyssinica are small oil seeds derived from the Niger plant. In India certain tribal committee used for niger seed oil is cooking purposes.

The oil extracted from niger seeds is known for its high smoke point which makes it suitable for various culinary applications. It is cultivated as a kharif crop and centre releases a Minimum Support Price (MSP) based on cost of production and market demand.

Niger seeds are primarily grown in Ethiopia and other parts of Africa. They are also cultivated in other countries like India, Nepal and Myanmar.

12 **Which one of the following best describes the concept of 'Small Farmer Large Field'?**

(Chap 2, Class-XI, New NCERT), (IAS Pre 2023)

(a) Resettlement of a large number of people, uprooted from their countries due to war, by giving them a large cultivable land which they cultivate collectively and share the produce

(b) Many marginal farmers in an area organise themselves into groups and synchronise and harmonise selected agricultural operations.

(c) Many marginal farmers in an area together make a contract with a corporate body and surrender their land to the corporate body for a fixed term for which the corporate body makes a payment of agreed amount to the farmers

(d) A company extends loans, technical knowledge and material inputs to a number of small farmers in an area so that they produce the agricultural commodity required by the company manufacturing process commercial production for its and

Ans. (b)

Exp. 'Small Farmer Large Field' (SFLF) is a collective action that aims to improve the livelihood of small and marginal farmers by overcoming the disadvantage they face due to lack of bargaining power in the supply chain.

It is participatory and flexible and allows small farmers to benefit from achieving economies of scale by organising themselves into groups and synchronising and harmonising selected operations. The model was effective in improving the livelihoods of small farmers.

13 **Consider the following statements.**

(Chap 2, Class-XI, New NCERT)

1. India has more arable area than China.
2. The proportion of irrigated area is more in India as compared to China.
3. The average productivity per hectare in Indian agriculture is higher than that in China.

How many of the above statements is/are correct?

(a) Only one
(b) Only two
(c) All three
(d) None of the above

Ans. (a)

Exp. Only one statement i.e., (1) is correct as India has the largest cropland of any country at 179.8 million hectares compared with 167.8 million in the US and 165.2 million in China.

Statements (2) and (3) are incorrect because China stands with the largest irrigated area, 69.1 as compared to 67 million hectare in India.

India's crop yields are lower than those in the US, Europe and China. The productivity of various crops and legumes in the country is less as compared to that of some countries in Europe, the US and China.

14 **With reference to India's food policy, consider the following statements.** *(Chap 4, Class-IX, New NCERT)*

1. It seeks to avert famines by maintaining a buffer stock.
2. It ensures remunerative price for the farmers so that they do not switch crops.
3. It encourages surplus production for the export market.
4. It aims to maintain general price line.

Which of the statements given above is/are correct?
(a) 1, 2, 3 and 4 (b) 1 and 4 (c) 1, 2 and 4 (d) 1 and 2

Ans. (b)

Exp. Statements (1) and (4) are correct with reference to food policy.

India's food policy seeks to avert famines by maintaining buffer stocks and management of scarcity through distribution of food grains at affordable price through Public Distribution System (PDS).

India's food policy aims to maintain general price level by buying and storing stocks of grain at times of good harvests to prevent prices falling below a target range So, it neutralises the fluctuation in production of a given crop, so that the prices may remain stable.

Statements (2) and (3) are incorrect because government ensures remunerative price for the farmers to get fair prices on crop not for switching crops. And it does not encourages surplus production for the export market.

15 **Which of the following are the features of Indian agriculture?** *(Chap 1, Class-IX, New NCERT)*

1. Disguised unemployment
2. High productivity
3. Majority of large farmers
4. Dependent on monsoon

Codes
(a) 1 and 2 (b) 2 and 4
(c) 2 and 3 (d) 1 and 4

Ans. (d)

Exp. Disguised unemployment and dependency on Monsoon are the features of Indian agriculture.

Features of Indian Agriculture are

Subsistence Agriculture It occurs when farmers grow crops to meet the needs of themselves and their families on small holdings.

Dependence on Monsoon Agriculture in India mainly depends on monsoon. If monsoon is good, the production will be more and if monsoon is less than average than the crops fail.

Disguished Unemployment It is primarily traced to the agricultural and unorganised sectors of the economy. In India Agriculture compose nearly half the labour force. This is mainly due to disguished unemployment.

Small Size of Holdings Due to large scale sub-division and fragmentation of holdings. Land holding size is quite small.

Low Agricultural Production Agricultural production is Low in India.

Traditional Methods of Production Methods of production of agriculture along with equipment are traditional. It is due to poverty and illiteracy of people. Traditional technology is the main cause of low production.

16 **Consider the following statements with respect to famine.** *(Chap 4, Class-IX, New NCERT)*

1. A famine is widespread scarcity of food, caused by several factors including war, natural disasters, crop failure, etc.
2. The most devastating famine that occurred in India was the Famine of Bengal in 1943.

Which of the statements given above is/are correct?
(a) Only 1 (b) Only 2
(c) Both 1 and 2 (d) Neither 1 nor 2

Ans. (c)

Exp. Both the statements (1) and (2) are correct with respect to famine.

A famine is a condition of scarcity of food in which deaths are caused due to hunger. This situation can be caused by many reasons such as a war, natural disaster, crop failure, drought, pandemic, etc.

The most devastating famine that occurred in India was the Famine of Bengal in 1943. This famine killed around thirty lakh people in the province of Bengal. The agricultural labourers, fisherman, transport workers, etc were most adversely affected by this famine.

17 **With reference to organic farming in India, consider the following statements.** *(Chap 6, Class-XI, New NCERT)*

1. The National Programme for Organic Production (NPOP) is operated under the guidelines and directions of the Union Ministry of Rural Development.
2. The Agricultural and Processed Food Products Export Development Authority (APEDA) functions as the Secretariat for the implementation of NPOP.
3. Sikkim has become India's first fully organic state.

Which of the statements given above is/are correct?
(a) 1 and 2 (b) 2 and 3 (c) Only 3 (d) Only 1

Ans. (b)

Exp. Statements (2) and (3) are correct with reference to organic farming in India.

Organic farming is a production system that avoids the use of synthetically compounded fertilisers pesticides, growth regulators, genetically modified organisms and livestock food additives.

APEDA functions as the Secretariat for the implementation of NPOP and Sikkim becomes the first fully organic State of India.

Statement (1) is incorrect because Ministry of Commerce has implemented the National Program for Organic Production (NPOP) since 2001.

18 **Consider the following statements.**

(Chap 4, Class-IX, New NCERT)

1. National Agricultural Insurance Scheme (NAIS) was launched in the Sixth Five Year Plan of the Indian Economy.
2. The growth rate of the primary sector of the Indian Economy sector never reached 8% during the planning history of Indian Economy.

Which of the statements given above is/are correct?

(a) Only 1 (b) Only 2
(c) Both 1 and 2 (d) Neither 1 nor 2

***Ans.* (b)**

Exp. Only statement (2) is correct as the growth rate of the primary sector of the Indian Economy sector reached 8% during the planning history of Indian Economy.

Statement (1) is incorrect because National Agricultural Insurance Scheme (NAIS) or Rashtriya Krishi Bima Yojana (RKBY) was launched in 1999-2000 during the Ninth Five Year Plan. NAMS envisages coverage of all food crops (cereals and pulses), oilseeds, horticultrual and commercial crops.

19 **Consider the following statements with respect to Pradhan Mantri Kisan Sampada Yojana (PMKSY).**

(Chap 4, Class-IX, New NCERT)

1. It is an umbrella scheme incorporating ongoing schemes like integrated cold chain and value addition infrastructure. Food safety and quality assurance infrastructure etc.
2. The scheme will be implemented by the Ministry of Agriculture.
3. It will help in providing better prices to farmers and is a big step towards doubling farmer's income.

How many of statements given above are correct?

(a) Only one (b) Only two
(c) All three (d) None of these

***Ans.* (b)**

Exp. Only two statements i.e., (1) and (3) are correct as Pradhan Mantri Kisan Sampada Yojana (PMKSY) launched in 2017-18 across the country. It is a comprehensive package aiming to create modern infrastructure with efficient supply chain management from farm gate to retail outlet.

The scheme boosts the growth of the food processing sector in the country and, helps in providing better prices to farmers, creates huge employment opportunities especially in the rural areas reduces wastage of agricultural produce, increases the processing level and enhances the export of the processed foods. Statement (2) is incorrect because the scheme will be implemented by the Ministry of Food Processing Industries (MoFPI).

20 **Consider the following statements.**

(Chap 6, Class-XI, New NCERT)

Statement-I In organic farming, only insecticides are added and no pesticide is used.

Statement-II No genetic modification is done to increase the yield of the crop.

Which one of the following is correct in respect of the above statements?

(a) Both Statement-I and Statement-II are correct and Statement-II is the correct explanation for Statement-I.
(b) Both Statement-I and Statement-II are correct and Statement-II is not the correct explanation for Statement-I.
(c) Statement-I is correct but statement-II is incorrect.
(d) Statement-I is incorrect but statement-II is correct.

***Ans.* (b)**

Exp. Both Statement-I and Statement-II are correct and Statement-II is not the correct explanation for Statement-I.

In organic farming, bio-pesticides derived from plants like neem, custard apple, and garlic. These natural extracts are prepared and used as deterrents against pests. They are safe for the environment, humans, and beneficial insects. Some useful microbes used as bio-fertilisers are bacteria, algae, and fungi.

Genetically modified plants are plants which have desirable characters such as resistance to pest, insects, droughts, and salinity organic farming involves the use of natural wild-type plants.

21 **Consider the following Assertion (A) and Reason (R) and choose the correct code.**

(Chap 4, Class-IX, New NCERT)

Assertion (A) The rising Minimum Support Prices (MSP) have raised the maintenance cost of procuring food grains for the government.

Reason (R) Rising transportation and storage costs of the FCI are other contributing factors in this increase.

Codes

(a) Both A and R are true and R is the correct explanation of A.
(b) Both A and R are true, but R is not the correct explanation of A.
(c) A is true, but R is false.
(d) A is false, but R is true.

***Ans.* (b)**

Exp. Both Assertion (A) and Reason (R) are true, but Reason (R) is not the correct explanation of Assertion (A).

The rising Minimum Support Price (MSP) have raised the maintenance cost of procuring foodgrains for the government. The increased foodgrains procurement at enhanced MSP is the result of the pressure exerted by leading foodgrain producing states such as Punjab, Haryana, Andhra Pradesh, etc.

Rising transportation and storage costs of the Food Corporation of India (FCI) are other contributing factors in this increase. The storage of massive food stocks has been responsible for high carrying costs, in addition to wastage and deterioration in grain quality.

22 Consider the following statements about buffer stock. *(Chap 4, Class-IX, New NCERT)*

1. Buffer Stock is the stock of foodgrains, namely wheat and jowar, procured by the government through the FCI.
2. The FCI purchases wheat and rice from the farmers in states where there is surplus production.

Which of the statements given above is/are incorrect?

(a) Only 1 (b) Only 2
(c) Both 1 and 2 (d) Neither 1 nor 2

Ans. (a)

Exp. Statement (1) is incorrect about buffer stock because it is the stock of foodgrains, namely wheat and rice (not jowar), procured by government through Food Corporation of India (FCI).

A buffer stock is maintained to distribute the procured foodgrain in the food-deficit areas and for the poors through ration shops. It is also maintained to deal with any unprecedented situation like crop failure.

23 Consider the following statements. *(Chap 4, Class-IX, New NCERT)*

1. Subsidy is a payment that a government makes to a producer to supplement the market price of a commodity.
2. Subsidies can keep consumer prices high while maintaining a higher income for domestic producers.

Which of the statements given above is/are correct?

(a) Only 1 (b) Only 2
(c) Both 1 and 2 (d) Neither 1 nor 2

Ans. (a)

Exp. Only statement (1) is correct as subsidy is a payment that a government makes to a producer to supplement the market price of a commodity. It leads to a fall in the price of the subsidised product. The objective of subsidy is to encourage the welfare of the society.

Statement (2) is incorrect because subsidies can keep consumer prices low (not high) while maintaining a higher income for domestic producers by increasing compitativeness of the product.

24 Consider the following Assertion (A) and Reason (R) and choose the correct code. *(Chap 2, Class-XI, New NCERT)*

Assertion (A) Fertiliser and pesticide subsidies result in overuse of resources which can be harmful to the environment.

Reason (R) Subsidies provide an incentive for wasteful use of resources.

Codes

(a) Both A and R are true and R is the correct explanation of A.
(b) Both A and R are true, but R is not the correct explanation of A.
(c) A is true, but R is false.
(d) A is false, but R is true.

Ans. (a)

Exp. Both Assertion (A) and Reason (R) are true and Reason (R) is the correct explanation of Assertion (A). Fertiliser and pesticide subsidies were given by the government to provide an incentive for adoption of new HYV technology by farmers.

Therefore, subsidies were needed to encourage farmers to test the new technology.

However, fertilisers and pesticides subsidies result in overuse of resources which can be harmful to the environment. Chemical fertilisers pollute the environment as well as reduce soil fertility.

Subsidies provide an incentive for overuse, which lead to wasteful use of resources.

25 Which of the following factors/policies were affecting the price of rice in India in the recent past? *(Chap 4, Class-IX, New NCERT)* *(IAS Pre 2020)*

1. Minimum Support Price 2. Government's trading
3. Government's stockpiling 4. Consumer subsidies

Codes

(a) 1, 2 and 4 (b) 1, 3 and 4
(c) 2 and 3 (d) 1, 2, 3 and 4

Ans. (d)

Exp. All of the given factors/policies were affecting the price of rice in India in the recent past.

The Minimum Support Price and consumer subsidies through Public Distribution System (PDS) tend to artificially increase or decrease the price of rice.

Government's trading and stockpiling tend to inflate the price of rice regardless of its condition of demand and supply.

Subsidies given by government through various food distribution schemes impact the price in the market directly or indirectly.

26 Consider the following statements. *(Chap 4, Class-IX, New NCERT)*

1. Pradhan Mantri Fasal Bima Yojana replaced the MNAIS and NAIS.
2. PM-KISAN is being implemented by the Ministry of Agriculture and farmers welfare.

Which of the statements given above is/are correct?

(a) Only 1
(b) Only 2
(c) Both 1 and 2
(d) Neither 1 nor 2

Ans. (c)

Exp. Both the statements (1) and (2) are correct as Pradhan Mantri Fasal Bima Yojana (PMFBY) was launched in 2016. It replaced the National Agricultural Insurance Scheme (NAIS) and Modified National Agricultural Insurance Scheme (MNAIS).

It aims to provide a comprehensive insurance cover against the failure of the crop thus helping in stabilising the income of the farmers.

Pradhan Mantri Kisan Samman Nidhi (PM-KISAN) was launched in February 2019. It is a Central Sector Scheme. It is being implemented by the Ministry of Agriculture and Farmers' Welfare.

Under the scheme, the Central Government transfers an amount of ₹ 6,000 per year, in 3 equal installments, directly into the bank accounts of all landholding farmers irrespective of the size of their landholdings.

27 Consider the following statements.

(Chap 6, Class-XI, New NCERT)

1. TRIFED is a national level apex organisation functioning under the administrative control of the Ministry of Tribal Affairs.
2. The AGMARKNET is a G2C e-governance portal.
3. ICAR is headquartered at Mumbai.
4. FAO is one of the UN Food Aid Organisations based in Rome (Italy).

Which of the statements given above is/are correct?

(a) 1, 2 and 3
(b) 1, 2 and 4
(c) 2, 3 and 4
(d) 1, 2, 3 and 4

Ans. (b)

Exp. Statements (1), (2) and (4) are correct. Tribal Cooperative Marketing Development Federation of India (TRIFED) came into existence in 1987. It is a National level apex organisation functioning under the Ministry of Tribal Affairs. Its head office is located in New Delhi.

The AGMARKNET is a Government to Citizen (G2C) e-governance portal. It caters to the needs of various Stakeholders such as farmers, industry, policy makers and academic institutions by providing agricultural marketing related information from a single window.

Statement (3) is incorrect because the Indian Council for Agricultural Research (ICAR) was established on 16th July, 1929. It is headquartered at New Delhi not in Mumbai.

Food and Agriculture Organisation (FAO) is a specialised agency of the United Nation. It is one of the UN food aid organisations based in Rome (Italy).

28 Consider the following statements regarding horticulture. *(Chap 6, Class-XI, New NCERT)*

1. The Horticulture sector contributes nearly one-third of the value of agricultural output and 6% of Gross Domestic Product of India.
2. Flower harvesting, nursery maintenance, hybrid seed production and tissue culture, propagation of fruits, flowers and food processing are covered under Horticulture sector.

Which of the statements given above is/are correct?

(a) Only 1 (b) Only 2
(c) Both 1 and 2 (d) Neither 1 nor 2

Ans. (c)

Exp. Both the statements (1) and (2) are correct regarding horticulture.

Horticulture sector contributes nearly one-third of the value of agricultural output and 6% of GDP of India.

India has emerged as a world leader in producing variety of fruits like mangoes, bananas, coconuts, cashew nuts and a number of spices. It is also the second largest producer of fruits and vegetables.

Flowers harvesting, nursery maintenance, hybrid seed production and tissue culture, propagation of fruits, flowers and food processing are covered under Horticulture sector. Horticulture sector not only play a vital role in providing food and nutrition but also address the employment concern.

29 Which of the following statements is/are correct?

(Chap 6, Class-XI, New NCERT)

(a) Sikkim became the first state in the world to be fully organic in 2016.
(b) Mission Organic Value Chain Development for North-East Region is a sub-mission under NMSA.
(c) Under PKVY, organic farming is promoted through adoption of organic villages by cluster approach.
(d) All of the above

Ans. (d)

Exp. All the above statements (a), (b) and (c) are correct. Sikkim became the first state in the world to be fully organic in 2016. North-East India has traditionally been organic and the consumption of chemical is far less than the rest of the country.

Mission Organic Value Chain Development for North-East Region (MOVCD-NER) is a Central Sector Scheme, a sub-mission under National Mission for Sustainable Agriculture (NMSA).

Paramparagat Krishi Vikas Yojana (PKVY) was launched in 2015. Under PKVY, organic farming is promoted through adoption of organic village by cluster approach and Participatory Guarantee System (PGS) Certification.

30 Consider the following statements.

(Chap 8, Class-XI, Tamil Nadu Board)

1. The target of second Green Revolution was to increase 400 million tonnes of food grain production.
2. This is to be achieved by 2020.

Which of the statements given above is/are correct?

(a) Only 1 (b) Only 2
(c) Both 1 and 2 (d) Neither 1 nor 2

Ans. (c)

Exp. Both the statements (1) and (2) are correct regarding Second Green Revolution as the target of Second Green Revolution was to increase 400 million tonnes of foodgrain production as against about 214 million tonnes in 2006-07. This is to be achieved by 2020. In agricultural sector, the growth rate of 5% and 6% has to be maintained over next 15 years.

Chapter 07

Industry and Industrial Policies

Industry and Industrial Policies

Industry

Introduction
- Manufacture of goods in factories
- Natural products are changed into other forms

Industrial Sectors in India
- **Public Sector** All enterprises under government; e.g. railway, postal
- **Private Sector** Private ownership; e.g. Tata Iron and Steel Company Limited
- **Joint Sector** Partnership between Private and Public Sector; e.g. Dutt Committee

Measure of Industrial Production
- **Purchasing Manager's Index** (PMI)
  - An indicator of business activity in manufacturing and services sector
  - PMI is a number from 0 to 100
- **Annual Survey of Industries** (ASI)
  - Calculated on annual basis
  - ASI data is based on the actual book of accounts
- **Index of Industrial Production** (IIP)
  - It helps us understand the growth of various sector
  - IIP is published monthly

Industrial Policy (Essential for Industrial Growth)

Industrial Policy Resolution, 1948
- Announced on 6th April, 1948 by then Industrial Minister late Shyama Prasad Mukherjee
- Defined the broad contours of the policy delineating the role of a nation
- The Industries (Development and Regulation)

Industrial Policy Resolution, 1956
- Regarded as the Economic Constitution of India
- Mainly emphasised the need to expand the public sector
- It provided the basic framework for government's policy till June, 1991

Industrial Policy, 1977
- Announced on 23rd December, 1977 by Janata Government led by Morarji Desai

Industrial Policy, 1991
- Announced in 1991 by Government of India
- Objective was to raise efficiency and economic growth

Public Sector Undertaking PSU)

Introduction
- A government owned corporation
- Equity of such companies owned by the government
  (i) Maharatna (13) – ONGC, NTPC
  (ii) Navratna (16) – BEL, HAIL, etc.
  (iii) Miniratna (74) – BEML, Goa shipyard, etc.

Large Scale Industries
- Referred to those industries, having huge infrastructure, high manpower
- Basic industries
- Capital goods industries
- Intermediate goods industries
- Consumer goods industries

Micro, Small and Medium Enterprises (MSME)
- Have been accepted as the engine of economic growth
- MSME Bill, 2018 proposes to reclassify all MSME

Importance of MSME
- Employment – Contribution to GDP
- Exports – Inclusive Growth
- Financial inclusion – Promote Innovation

SOURCE *Old NCERT Class IX & X (Towards Economic Development), Old NCERT Class IX & X (The State and Economic Development), New NCERT Class XI (Indian Economy on the Eve of Independence), New NCERT Class XI (Indian Economy 1950–1990), New NCERT Class XI (Liberalisation, Privatisation and Globalisation : An Appraisal)*

1 **Consider the following statements.**
(Chap 4, Class-IX & X, Old NCERT)

Statement-I Labour intensitve refers to a process or industry that requires a large amount of labour to produce its goods or services.

Statement-II They are generally found in developing countries where availability of semi-skilled workforce is high.

Which one of the following is correct in respect of the above statements?

(a) Both Statement-I and Statement-II are correct and Statement-II is the correct explanation for Statement-I.
(b) Both Statement-I and Statement-II are correct and Statement-II is not the correct explanation for Statement-I.
(c) Statement-I is correct but Statement-II is incorrect.
(d) Statement-I is incorrect but Statement-II is correct.

Ans. (a)

Exp. Both Statement-I and Statement-II are correct and Statement-II is the correct explanation for Statement-I.

Labour intensive industries are those that require a significant amount of human labour to produce goods or services. The higher the proportion of labour costs required, the more labour-intensive the business.

They are generally found in developing countries where availability of semi-skilled workforce is high.

For example, bidi industry, bangle industry, textile industry, etc.

2 **Consider the following statements.**
(Chap 1, Class-XI, New NCERT)

1. Industries which can produce machine tools, which is used for producing article for current consumption are known as capital goods.
2. All durable good like cars, trucks, refrigerates buildings, air crafts, air fields and sub-marine are capital goods product.
3. Capital goods are differ from consumer goods, which are the end product of production and manufacturing.

How many of the above statements is/are correct?

(a) Only one
(b) Only two
(c) All three
(d) None of these

Ans. (c)

Exp. All three statements i.e., (1), (2) and (3) are correct as capital goods are physical assets a company uses to produce goods and services for consumers. It include fixed assets, such as buildings, machinery, equipment, vehicles and tools. Capital goods differ from consumer goods, which are the end product of production and manufacturing.

3 **Consider the following statements regarding iron and steel industry.** *(Chap 1, Class-XI New NCERT)*

1. Large scale iron and steel production was started in 1907 by TISCO established at Jamshedpur.
2. In 1919, Indian Iron and Steel Company (IISCO) was established at Burnpur. Both TISCO and IISCO are private sector companies.
3. The first public sector company was Vishwashwaraiya Iron and Steel Works at Bhadravati.

How many of the above statements is/are correct?

(a) Only one (b) Only two
(c) All three (d) None of these

Ans. (c)

Exp. All three statements i.e., (1), (2) and (3) are correct regarding iron and steel industry. The first steel plant in India was set-up in India at Jamshedpur. It was established by Jamshedji Nusserwanji Tata in 1907.

IISCO was established in 1919 at Hirapur later to be called Burnpur in West Bengal. Both TISCO and IISCO are private sector companies.

The first public sector company was 'Vishwashwaraiya Iron and Steel works' at Bhadravati, Karnataka. It was founded on 18th January, 1923 as the 'Mysore Iron works' by M. Visvesvaraya. Since 1989, it works under the Jurisdiction of the Steel Authority of India Limited.

4 **Consider the following statements about the Industrial policy of India.** *(Chap 3, Class-XI, New NCERT)*

1. Industrial Policy Resolution of 1948 classified industries of India into 15 broad areas.
2. Industrial Policy of 1956 provided the basic framework for the government's policy in regard to industries till June 1990.

Which of the statement(s) given above is/are incorrect?

(a) Only 1
(b) Only 2
(c) Both 1 and 2
(d) Neither 1 nor 2

Ans. (c)

Exp. Both the statements (1) and (2) are incorrect about the Industrial Policy of India. The Industrial Policy Resolution, 1948 is the first industrial policy announced in April 1948.

Industries classified into four categories viz, Public sector, Mixed sector, Controlled private sector and Private and Cooperative sector.

Industrial Policy of 1956 provided the basic framework for the government's policy in regard to industries till June 1991. Industrial Policy of 1956 was regarded as the Economic Constitution of India or the Bible of State Capitalism.

5 **Consider the following statements regarding small scale industries.** *(Chap 2, Class-XI, New NCERT)*

1. A 'Small-scale industry' is defined with reference to the maximum investment allowed on the assets of a unit.
2. At present, the maximum investment allowed is ₹ 5 crores.

Which of the statement(s) given above is/are correct?

(a) Only 1 (b) Only 2
(c) Both 1 and 2 (d) Neither 1 nor 2

***Ans.* (a)**

Exp. Only statement (1) is correct regarding small scale industries. A 'Small-scale industry' is defined with reference to the maximum investment allowed on the assets of a unit. This limit has changed over a period of time. In 1950, a small scale industrial unit was one which invested a maximum of ₹ 5 lakh.

Statement (2) is incorrect because as per new definition, small scale industrial unit is one with an investment of not more than ₹ 10 crore and a turnover of ₹ 50 crore.

It is believed that small scale industries are more 'labour intensive' i.e. they use more labour than the large scale industries and therefore, generate more employment.

6 **With reference to Industrial Policy of 1991, consider the following statements.** *(Chap 8, Class-XI, Tamil Nadu Board)*

1. It reduced Government stakes in Public Sector Enterprises.
2. It led to increased competition, that led to lower prices in many goods.
3. This was the first Industrial policy in which foreign companies were allowed to have a majority stake in India.

How many of the above statements is/are correct?

(a) Only one (b) Only two
(c) All three (d) None of these

***Ans.* (c)**

Exp. All three statements i.e., (1), (2) and (3) are correct with reference to the Industrial Policy of 1991.

As a result of the Industrial Policy of 1991, Government stakes in Public Sector Enterprises were reduced to enhance their efficiency and competitiveness. It led to the disinvestment of public sector.

The Industrial Policy of 1991 provided easier entry of multinational companies, privatisation, removal of asset limit on MRTP companies, and allowed liberal licensing which increased the competition and that led to lowering of prices in many goods such as electronics prices.

This was the first industrial policy in which foreign companies were allowed to have a majority stake in India. In 47 high priority industries, upto 51% FDI was allowed. For export trading houses, FDI up to 74% was allowed. This led to the liberalisation of foreign investment.

7 **Consider the following statements regarding the concept of Economic reform.** *(Chap 3, Class-XI, New NCERT)*

1. It is safer to see economic reform as a policy shift in an economy from one to another or 'alternative development strategies'.
2. Economic reforms denote the process in which a government prescribes declining role for state and expanding role for the private sector in an economy.

Which of the following statement(s) is/are correct?

(a) Only 1 (b) Only 2
(c) Both 1 and 2 (d) Neither 1 nor 2

***Ans.* (b)**

Exp. Only statement (2) is correct regarding economic reform. Economic reforms denote the process in which a government prescribes declining role for state and expanding role for the private sector in an economy. It had three main objectives-Liberalisation, Privatisation and Globalisation (LPG).

These reforms aimed to enhance the cooperation of the private sector in the growth of the Indian economy. It also led to a decrease in the government's role in the industrial units within the country.

Statement (1) is incorrect because it is not safer to see economic reform as a policy shift in an economy from one to another or 'alternative development strategies'.

8 **Consider the following factors.** *(Chap 3, Module-2, NIOS)*

1. High investment in industries
2. Expanding market for product
3. Dynamic entrepreneurship

Which of the above is/are required for accelerated growth of an economy?

(a) Only 1 (b) 1 and 2 (c) 1, 2 and 3 (d) 2 and 3

***Ans.* (c)**

Exp. All the above factors are required for accelerated growth of an economy.

High investment in industries are directly accelerated to growth of an economy.

Market expansion is growth strategy that aims to make a product or service available in new market.

Dynamic entrepreneurship promotes innovation and competition, leading to new and improved products thats contribute to economic growth.

9 **Consider the following factors regarding an industry.** *(Chap 3, Module-2, NIOS)*

1. Capital investments 2. Business turnover
3. Labour forces 4. Power consumption

Which of the following factors determine the nature and size of the industry?

(a) 1, 3 and 4 (b) 1, 2 and 4 (c) 2, 3 and 4 (d) 2 and 3

***Ans.* (a)**

Exp. Among the given factors, (1), (3) and (4) determines the nature and size of the industry.

Capital Investments Capital investment helps the entrepreneur to make business grow to a big size.

Availability of Labour If the labour forces is not available in the business then business would not grow.

Power Consumption Industry uses fossil fuels and renewable energy sources.

Different industries have vastly different energy needs which determine the nature and size of the industry.

10 **Consider the following statements.**

(Chap 8, Class-XI, Tamil Nadu Board) (Chap 3, Module-2, NIOS)

1. The Index of Industrial Production (IIP) is an index that indicates the performance of various industrial sectors of the Indian economy.
2. It is a short term indicator of industrial growth.
3. IIP is published monthly and six weeks after the reference month ends.

How many of the above statements is/are correct?

(a) Only one (b) Only two
(c) All three (d) None of these

Ans. (c)

Exp. All three statements i.e., (1), (2) and (3) are correct as IIP is an index which helps us understand the growth of various sectors in the Indian economy such as mining, electricity and manufacturing.

It is short term indicator of industrial growth till the results from annual Survey of Industries (ASI) and National Accounts Statistics (e.g GDP) are available.

Index of Industrial production (IIP) is released by the National Statistics Office (NSO) of the Ministry of Statistics and programme implementation. It is published monthly and six weeks after the reference month ends.

11 **Consider the following Assertion (A) and Reason (R) and choose the correct code.**

(Chap 2, Class-XI, New NCERT)

Assertion (A) The excessive regulation of industries came to be called as the License Permit Raj, prevented certain firms from becoming more efficient.

Reason (R) More time was spent by industrialists in trying to obtain a license or lobby with the concerned ministries rather than on thinking about how to improve their products.

Codes

(a) Both A and R are true and R is the correct explanation of A.
(b) Both A and R are true, but R is not the correct explanation of A.
(c) A is true, but R is false.
(d) A is false, but R is true.

Ans. (a)

Exp. Both Assertion (A) and Reason (R) are true and Reason (R) is the correct explanation of Assertion (A).

The excessive regulation of industries came to be called as the License Permit Raj, prevented certain firms from becoming more efficient. It is because the need to obtain a license to start an industry was misused by industrial houses. A big industrialists would get license not for starting a new firm but to prevent competitors from starting new firms.

More time was spent by industrialists in trying to obtain a license or lobby with the concerned ministries rather than on thinking about how to improve their products.

12 **Consider the following statements about deregulation of the industrial sector.**

(Chap 3, Class-XI, New NCERT)

1. Industrial licensing was abolished for almost all except alcohols, cigarettes, hazardous chemicals, industrial explosives, electronics, aerospace, drugs and pharmaceuticals.
2. The only industries which are now reserved for the public sector are a part of atomic energy generation and some core activities in railway transport.

Which of the statement(s) given above is/are incorrect?

(a) Only 1 (b) Only 2
(c) Both 1 and 2 (d) Neither 1 nor 2

Ans. (d)

Exp. Neither statement (1) nor (2) is incorrect about deregulation of the industrial sector.

The reform policies introduced in and after 1991 removed many of the trade restrictions. Industrial licensing was abolished for almost all but for product categories like alcohols, cigarettes, hazardous chemicals, industrial explosives, electronics, aerospace, drugs and pharmaceuticals. The only industries which are now reserved for public sector are a part of atomic energy generation and some core activities in railway transport.

13 **Consider the following heavy industries.**

(Chap 1, Class-XI, New NCERT) (IAS Pre 2023)

1. Fertiliser plants 2. Oil refineries 3. Steel plants

Green hydrogen is expected to play a significant role in decarbonizing, how many to the above industries?

(a) Only one (b) Only two
(c) All three (d) None of these

Ans. (c)

Exp. Green hydrogen can play a significant role in decarbonizing all of the above mentioned heavy industries i.e., fertiliser plants, oil refiners and steel plants.

By using green hydrogen as a clean energy source, fertiliser plants can reduce their carbon emissions. Green hydrogen can be used to generate electricity or directly as a feedstock in the ammonia production process, which is a key component of fertiliser manufacturing.

Green hydrogen can be utilised in oil refineries to replace or supplement fossil fuels, reducing their carbon footprint.

Green hydrogen can be used as a reducing agent in the steelmaking process, replacing coal or coke. This process, know as direct reduction, enables the production of 'green' or low-carbon steel.

14 **Which of the following industries fall under the purview of industrial licensing that requires compulsory licensing?** *(Chap 3, Class-XI, New NCERT)*

1. Industrial explosive
2. Hazardous chemicals
3. Cigars and cigarettes of tobacco
4. Animal fats and oil

Codes

(a) 1, 2 and 4 (b) 1, 2 and 3
(c) 2, 3 and 4 (d) 1, 2, 3 and 4

Ans. (b)

Exp. Options (1), (2) and (3) falls under the purview of industrial licensing that require compulsory licensing. There are only 4 industries at present related to security, strategic and environmental concerns, where an industrial licence is currently required. These are

- Electronic aerospace and defiance equipment.
- Specified hazardous chemicals.
- Industrial explosives.
- Cigars and cigarettes of tobacco and manufactured tobacco substitutes.

15 **Consider the following objectives of the Trade Policy Reforms after 1991.** *(Chap 3, Class-XI, New NCERT)*

1. Dismantling of qualitative restrictions on imports and exports.
2. Reduction of tariff rates.
3. Removal of licensing procedures for imports.

Which of the statement(s) given above is/are incorrect?

(a) Only 1 (b) Only 2
(c) 1, 2 and 3 (d) 1 and 3

Ans. (a)

Exp. Only statement (1) is incorrect regarding the objectives of the Trade Policy Reforms after 1991. The Trade Reforms after 1991 aimed at as dismantling of quantitative (not qualitative) restrictions on imports and exports.

Trade and Investment Policy Reforms were introduced to promote the efficiency of local industries and adoption of modern technologies.

In the light of trade policy reforms, import licensing was abolished and also export duties were removed.

16 **Consider the following pairs is/are correctly matched.** *(Chap 3, Class-XI, New NCERT)*

1. Maharatna – Steel Authority of India Limited
2. Navratna – Bharat Sanchar Nigam Limited
3. Miniratna – Mahanagar Telephone Nigam Limited

How many of the above pairs is/are incorrectly matched?

(a) Only one pair (b) Only two pairs
(c) All three pairs (d) None of the pairs

Ans. (b)

Exp. Only two pairs i.e., (2) and (3) are incorrectly matched.

Bharat Sanchar Nigam Limited (BSNL) comes under 'Miniratna' while Mahanagar Telephone Nigam Limited (MTNL) is a 'Navratna' company.

In order to improve efficiency, infuse professionalism and enable them to compete more effectively in the liberalised global environment, the government identifies PSEs and declare them as Maharatna, Navratnas and Miniratnas. They are given greater managerial and operational autonomy to run the company efficiently and increase their profits.

17 **Consider the following statements.** *(Chap 4, Class-IX & X, Old NCERT)*

1. MUDRA was launched by the government in 2015 for providing loans up to ₹ 10 lakh.
2. The programme Make in India started in September 2014.
3. AIM-iCREST programme launched by NITI Aayog.

Which of the statement(s) given above is/are correct?

(a) 1 and 2 (b) 1, 2 and 3
(c) 2 and 3 (d) None of these

Ans. (b)

Exp. All the statements (1), (2) and (3) are correct. MUDRA is financial institution set-up by the Government of India in 2015 for providing loan upto ₹ 10 lakh to the non-corporate, non-farms small-micro-enterprises.

The Make in India Campaign was launched by the Prime Minister of India on 25th September, 2014. Make in India Campaign aims at reviving the job creative manufacturing sector, which is being seen as the key to take the Indian economy on a sustainable high growth rate.

AIM-iCREST launched by Atal Innovation Mission is an Incubator Capabilities Enhancement Programme launched by NITI Aayog for a Robust Ecosystem focused on creating high performing startups.

Chapter 08

Money and Banking

Money and Banking

Inflation and Money

Inflation

- Refers to rise in the prices of most goods; Indicative of the decrease in the purchasing power of a unit of country's currency

Measures to Control

- **Monetary Measures** Credit contraction, Issue of new currency
- **Fiscal Measure** Increase in Direct tax, Price control

- Wholesale Price Index (WPI) Measures the changes in price of goods
- Consumer Price Index (CPI) Measures price changes from retail buyer

Types of Money

- **Actual Money** Metallic, Paper
- **Acceptable Money** Legal tender, Bank money, Credit money

Classification of Money on the Basis of Money Supply

- **Reserve Money** (M0)
  - Currency in Circulation + Bankers' deposits with RBI + Other deposits with RBI
- **Narrow Money** (M1)
  - Currency with public + Demand deposits with the Banking System (current account, saving account) + Other deposits with RBI
- **Broad Money** (M3)
  - M1 + Time deposits with the Banking System
  - M4 = M3 + All deposits with Post Office Savings Banks

Reserve Bank of India

Introduction

- RBI is the supreme monetary and banking authority
- Controls the banking system
- Keeps the reserve of all commercial banks
- It also has the responsibility protect market, for government securities and channelise credit for the purpose of investment in desired direction
- RBI was nationalised in 1949 and its first Indian Governor was CD Deshmukh

Functions

- Issue of currency notes
- Banker to other Banks
- Credit control function
- Banker to the government

Monetary Policy

- Economic and financial stability
- Flow of credits

Quantitative Instruments

- Cash Reserve Ratio (CRR)
- Statutory Liquidity Ratio (SLR)
- Open Market Operations

Qualitative Instruments

- Moral suasion
- Direct action
- Prompt corrective action

Banking Sector Reforms and Non-Banking Financial Companies

Banking Sector Reforms Committee

- Banking Sector Reforms
- Narasimham Committee Report I- 1991
- Narasimham Committee Report II- 1998
- Damodaran Committee - 2011
- Usha thorat Committee-2011
- MV Nair Committee- 2011
- Urjit Patel Committee-2013
- Nachiket Mor Committee-2013

Government Schemes

- Sovereign Gold Bond Scheme
- Mudra Bank
- Indradhanush Scheme 2015
- Financial Stability and Developed Council (FSDC)

Non-Banking Financial Companies

- Financial institutions that offer various banking services but don't have any legal licenses
- NBFC offer loans, credit facilities, currency exchange retirement planning, money markets and merger activities

Types / Categories

- Asset Finance Company (AFC)
- Loan Company (LC)
- Investment Company (IC)
- Infrastructure Finance Company (IFC)

SOURCE *Old NCERT Class IX & X (The Infrastructure of the Indian Economy), Old NCERT Class IX & X (The State and Economic Development), New NCERT Class X (Money and Credit), New NCERT Class XII (Money and Banking), Old NCERT Class XII (Money and Banking System Appendix)*

Money

1 **Consider the following statements regarding the barter system.** *(Chap 3, Class-IX & X, Old NCERT)*

1. Economic exchanges without the mediation of money are referred to as barter exchanges.
2. 'Double coincidence of wants' is absent in barter system.

Which of the statement(s) given above is/are incorrect?

(a) Only 1 (b) Only 2
(c) Both 1 and 2 (d) Neither 1 nor 2

Ans. (b)

Exp. Only statement (2) is incorrect regarding the barter system because barter system presumes the 'double coincidence of wants'.

It means for the completion of barter, both parties, the seller and buyers have to agree to sell and buy commodities from each other. There is no need of the mediation of money in barter exchange.

2 **With reference to 'function of money', which of the following statements are correct?** *(Chap 3, Class-XII, New NCERT)*

1. It acts as a medium of exchange.
2. It acts as a convenient unit of account.
3. It acts as a store of value.

Codes

(a) 1 and 2 (b) 2 and 3 (c) 1 and 3 (d) 1, 2 and 3

Ans. (d)

Exp. All the statements (1), (2) and (3) are correct regarding 'function of money'.

Money is the most liquid of all assets and is universally accepted, so it is used as a medium of exchange.

The value of all goods and services can be expressed in monetary units hence, it also serves as a convenient unit of account.

Further, money is not perishable and its storage cost is considerably lower. Thus, it can also act as a store of value for individuals.

3 **Consider the following statements about currency issued by Government of India.** *(Chap 3, Class-XII, New NCERT)*

1. The currency issued by the Government of India is primarily in the form of coins only.
2. The currency issued by the Government of India includes banknotes and coins, serving as legal tender for all transactions within the country.
3. The currency issued by the Government of India is exclusively in the form of banknotes.

Which of the statements given above is/are correct?

(a) 1 and 2 (b) Only 2
(c) 2 and 3 (d) All of these

Ans. (b)

Exp. Only statement (2) is correct about currency issued by Government of India. Government of India issued banknotes and coin, serving as legal tender for all transaction within the country. 1 rupee notes, 1 rupee coin and 50 paise coin issued by Government of India have legal tender within the country.

Statements (1) and (3) are incorrect because government issues not only coins but currency as well. It is not exclusively for government to issue banknotes only.

4 **Consider the following statements.** *(Chap 3, Class-XII, New NCERT)*

1. The Larger the quantum of transaction to be made, the larger is the quantity of money demanded.
2. When interest rates go up, people become more interested in holding money.
3. At the higher interest rates, money demanded comes down.

Which of the statements given above is/are incorrect?

(a) 1 and 2 (b) 2 and 3 (c) Only 2 (d) All of these

Ans. (c)

Exp. Only statement (2) is incorrect because when interest rates go up people become less interested in holding money.

It is because holding money amounts to holding less of interest-earning deposits, and thus less interest received. Therefore, the higher the interest rate, the more you must give up to hold money, so less money is held.

5 **If you withdraw ₹ 1,00,000 in cash from your Demand Deposit Account at your bank, what will be the immediate effect on aggregate money supply in the economy?** *(Chap 3, Class-XII, New NCERT) (IAS Pre 2020)*

(a) It will reduce it by ₹ 1,00,000.
(b) It will increase it by ₹ 1,00,000.
(c) It will increase it by more than ₹ 1,00,000.
(d) It will remain unchanged.

Ans. (d)

Exp. The immediate effect would be a no change in the aggregate money supply in the economy.

The aggregate money supply in an economy can be expressed as $M = C + D$,

wherein 'C' is Currency with public

'D' is Demand Deposits by public with banks.

Now taking out ₹ 1 lakh from 'D' would increase same amount 'C' with public which will not impact the overall supply of money. The money supply is the total value of money available in the economy at a point of time.

Banking

6 **Consider the following statements.** *(Chap 3, Class-XII, New NCERT), (IAS Pre 2018)*

1. The Reserve Bank of India manages and administers the securities of the Government of India, but not the securities of any State Government.

2. The Government of India issues treasury bills and the State Governments do not issue any treasury papers.
3. Treasury offers are issued at a discount to their par value.

Which of the statements given above is/are correct?

(a) 1 and 2 (b) Only 3 (c) 2 and 3 (d) All of these

Ans. (c)

Exp. Statements (2) and (3) are correct.

Treasury bills are issued by only Central Government of India and not by the State Government.

Treasury bills are issued through a competitive bidding process at a discount from par values, which means that rather than paying fixed interest payments like conventional bonds, the application of the bond provides the return to the holder.

Statement (1) incorrect because the Reserve Bank of India (RBI) manages and administers the securities of the Government of India and the securities of any State Government.

7 In India, which one of the following is responsible for maintaining price stability by controlling inflation? *(Chap 3, Class-XII, New NCERT), (IAS Pre 2022)*

(a) Department of Consumer Affairs
(b) Expenditure Management Commission
(c) Financial Stability and Development Council
(d) Reserve Bank of India

Ans. (d)

Exp. Reserve Bank of India is responsible for maintaining price stability by controlling inflation. While keeping in mind the objective of growth. Price stability is a necessary pre-condition to sustain growth. RBI uses various monetary policy tools to control inflation and ensure price stability. These include repo rate, reverse repo rate, bank rate, open market operations, Cash Reserve Ratio (CRR) Statutory Liquidity Ratio (SLR) and Liquidity Adjustment Facility (LAF).

8 Consider the following statements with respect to the Reserve Bank of India (RBI). *(Chap 3, Class-XII, New NCERT), (IAS Pre 2001)*

1. It is a banker to the Central Government.
2. It formulates and implements monetary policy.
3. It acts as an agent of the government in relation to the International Monetary Fund (IMF).
4. It operates the lending programme of the Government of India.

Which of the statements given above is/are correct?

(a) 1 and 2 (b) 3 and 4
(c) 2, 3 and 4 (d) All of these

Ans. (d)

Exp. All the given statements are correct with respect to RBI. The Reserve Bank of India (RBI) is the banker to the Central Government. The Reserve Bank of India (RBI) formulates and implements monetary policy in India. Monetary policy is the use of interest rates and other tools to control the money supply and inflation. The RBI uses monetary policy to achieve its objectives of price stability and financial stability.

The Reserve Bank of India (RBI) acts as an agent of the Government of India in relation to the International Monetary Fund (IMF) means that the RBI is responsible for representing the government of India at the IMF and for carrying out its instructions.

The Reserve Bank of India (RBI) operates the lending programme of the Government of India means that the RBI lends money to the government through treasury bills and bonds. The RBI also manages the government's cash and debt.

9 With reference to Cash Reserve Ratio (CRR), consider the following statements. *(Chap 3, Class-XII, New NCERT)*

1. CRR is the percentage of deposits which a bank must keep with itself in the form of any liquid asset.
2. Higher the CRR requirement, lower will be the credit creation in the economy.

Which of the statements given above is/are correct?

(a) Only 1 (b) Only 2
(c) Both 1 and 2 (d) Neither 1 nor 2

Ans. (b)

Exp. Only statement (2) is correct with reference to Cash Reserve Ratio (CRR). If the CRR requirement is higher, banks will have less money to lend, which would reduce the credit creation in the economy. Conversely, lowering the CRR would enable banks to lend more, thus potentially increasing credit creation.

Statement (1) is incorrect because CRR (Cash Reserve Ratio) is a percentage of a bank's deposits that must be held as reserves with the Central Bank.

10 Which of the following statements is/are correct regarding the Repo Rate? *(Chap 3, Class-XII, New NCERT)*

1. It is always lower than the Bank Rate.
2. It is always higher than Reverse Repo Rate.
3. It focuses on short term financial needs.
4. No collateral is involved when it is charged.

Select the correct answer using the codes given below.

(a) 1 and 2 (b) 1, 2 and 3
(c) 1 and 3 (d) All of these

Ans. (b)

Exp. Statements (1), (2) and (3) are correct with reference to the Repo Rate.

Repo Rate is always lower than the Bank Rate. Increase in Bank Rate directly affects the lending rates offered to the customer, restricting people to avail loans and damages the overall economic growth, whereas increase in Repo Rate is usually handled by the banks and doesn't affect customers directly.

Repo Rate is always higher than Reserve Repo Rate. A higher reverse Repo Rate would encourage banks to store funds with the RBI rather than make them available for lending.

Repo Rate loans are short-term borrowings and they focus on short term financial needs, with banks getting overnight or term funds while the RBI holds the securities.

Statement (4) is incorrect because no collateral is involved while charging Bank Rate but securities, bonds, agreements and collateral is involved when Repo Rate is charged.

11 If the RBI decides to adopt an Expansionist Monetary Policy, which of the following would it not do? *(Chap 3, Class-XII, New NCERT)*

1. Cut and optimise the Statutory Liquidity Ratio.
2. Increase the Marginal Standing Facility Rate.
3. Cut the Bank Rate and Repo Rate.

Codes

(a) 1 and 2 (b) Only 2
(c) 1 and 3 (d) All of these

Ans. (b)

Exp. If the RBI decides to adopt an Expansionist Monetary Policy, it would not do increase the Marginal Standing Facility Rate (MSFR).

Whereas, cut and optimise the Statutory Liquidity Ratio (SLR) and cut the Bank Rate and Repo Rate decided by RBI to adopt a Expansionist Monetary Policy.

12 Consider the following statements about the tools used by RBI to control money supply. *(Chap 3, Class-XII, New NCERT)*

1. Banks are required to keep some reserves in liquid form in the short term known as Liquidity Adjustment Facility (LAF).
2. Cash Reserve Ratio (CRR) is the percentage of deposits which a bank must keep as cash reserves with the bank.

Which of the statements given above is/are incorrect?

(a) Only 1
(b) Only 2
(c) Both 1 and 2
(d) Neither 1 nor 2

Ans. (a)

Exp. Only statement (1) is incorrect about the tools used by RBI to control money supply.

Banks are required to keep some reserves in liquid form in the short term. This ratio is called Statutory Liquidity Ratio (SLR) and not Liquidity Adjustment Facility (LAF). As of November, 2021, SLR is 18% on the other hand, Cash Reserve Ratio (CRR) is the percentage of deposits which a bank must keep as cash reserves with the bank. This is done to ensure that no bank is over lending. This is the legal requirement and is binding on the banks. As of November, 2021, CRR rate is 4%.

13 Consider the following statements. *(Chap 3, Class-XII, New NCERT)*

1. Qualitative tools control the extent of money supply by changing the CRR, or bank rate or open market operations.
2. Quantitative tools include persuasion by the Central Bank in order to make commercial banks discourage or encourage lending which is done through moral suasion, margin requirement, etc.

Which of the statements given above is/are incorrect?

(a) Only 1 (b) Only 2 (c) Both 1 and 2 (d) Neither 1 nor 2

Ans. (c)

Exp. Both the statements (1) and (2) are incorrect.

The tools used by the Central Bank can be qualitative or quantitative. Quantitative tools control the extent of money supply by changing the Cash Reserve Ratio (CRR) or bank rate or open market operations. It is used either to increase or decrease the supply of money in the economy.

Qualitative tools for controlling the money supply by the Central Bank include persuasion by the Central Bank in order to make commercial banks discourage or encourage lending which is done through moral suasion, margin requirement, etc.

14 Consider the following statements regarding the open market operations of the RBI. *(Chap 3, Class-XII, New NCERT)*

1. When RBI buys a Government bond in the open market, it pays for it by giving a cheque.
2. Selling of a bond by RBI leads to increase in quantity of reserves and hence the money supply.
3. RBI cannot sell bonds to the private institutions.

Which of the statements given above is/are correct?

(a) Only 1 (b) 2 and 3 (c) Only 3 (d) 1 and 2

Ans. (a)

Exp. Only statement (1) is correct regarding open market operations of the RBI. When RBI buys a Government bond in the open market, it pays for it by giving a cheque. This cheque increases the total amount of reserves in the economy and thus increases the money supply.

Statements (2) and (3) are incorrect because selling of a bond by RBI (to private individuals or institutions) leads to reduction in quantity of reserves and hence the money supply. RBI can sell bonds to the private institutions.

Open market operations refers to buying and selling of bonds issued by the Government in the open market. This purchase and sale is entrusted to the Central Bank on behalf of the Government.

15 The terms 'Marginal Standing Facility Rate' and 'Net Demand and Time Liabilities', sometimes appearing in news, are used in relation to *(Chap 3, Class-XII, New NCERT)*

(a) banking operation
(b) communication networking
(c) military strategies
(d) supply and demand of agricultural products

Ans. (a)

Exp. The terms 'Marginal Standing Facility Rate' (MSFR) and 'Net Demand and Time Liabilities' (NDTL) sometimes appearing in news, are used in relation to banking operations.

The Marginal Standing Facility Rate is the rate at which the Reserve Bank of India (RBI) lends money to commercial banks on an overnight basis against eligible securities, it is the highest rate at which banks can borrow money from the RBI.

Net Demand and Time Liabilities (NDTL) is a term used in banking to refer to the total amount of money that commercial banks owe to their customers. It is calculated by subtracting the amount of money that banks have deposited with the Central Bank from the total amount of money that they have lend to customers.

16 Which one of the following activities of the Reserve Bank of India is considered to be a part of 'sterilization'? *(Chap 3, Class-XII, New NCERT) (IAS Pre 2021)*

(a) Conducting Open Market Operations
(b) Oversight of settlement and payment systems
(c) Debt and cash management for the Central and State Governments
(d) Regulating the functions of Non-Banking Financial Institutions

Ans. (a)

Exp. Statement (a) is correct with reference to the activities of the Reserve bank of India which is considered to be a part of 'sterilization'. Open Market Operations (OMOs) are one of the tools used by the RBI for sterilization. OMOs are the purchase or sale of government securities by the Cenrtal Bank in the open market in order to regulate the money supply in the economy.

Sterilization is an action taken by the Central Bank (such as RBI in India) to counter balance the effects of foreign exchange interventions on domestic money supply and inflation. It is done to neutralise the impact of inflows or outflows of foreign exchange reserves on the domestic monetary system.

17 The money multiplier in an economy increases with which one of the following?

(Chap 3, Class-XII, New NCERT) (IAS Pre 2021)

(a) Increase in the cash reserve ratio.
(b) Increase in the banking habit of the population.
(c) Increase in the statutory liquidity ratio.
(d) Increase in the population of the country.

Ans. (b)

Exp. The money multipliers in an economy increases with increase in the banking habit of the population.

Money multiplier is defined as the ratio of the stock of money to the stock of high powered money in an economy. With increased banking habits, the deposits in the banking system will increase, which then will increase the money multiplier.

18 Consider the following statements.

(Chap 3, Class-XII, New NCERT)

1. The Central Bank may sell the securities through an agreement which has a specification about the date and price at which it will be repurchased called a reverse repurchase agreement or reverse repo.
2. The Reserve Bank of India conducts repo and reverse repo operations at various maturities i.e., overnight, 7 days, 14 days, etc.

Which of the statement(s) given above is/are correct?

(a) Only 1
(b) Only 2
(c) Both 1 and 2
(d) Neither 1 nor 2

Ans. (c)

Exp. Both the statements (1) and (2) are correct.

The Central Bank may sell the securities through an agreement which has a specification about the date and price at which it will be repurchased.

This type of agreement is called a reverse repurchase agreement or reverse repo. The rate at which the money is withdrawn in this manner is called as 'reverse repo rate'.

It is a type of open market operation and important tool to control the money supply. The present, reverse repo rate is 3.5%.

The Reserve Bank of India conducts repo and reverse repo operations at various maturities i.e., overnight, 7 days, 14 days, etc. This type of operations have now become the main tool of monetary policy of the RBI.

19 Consider the following statements regarding currency notes and coins. *(Chap 3, Class-XII, New NCERT)*

1. Currency notes and coins are called flat money.
2. They do not have intrinsic value like a gold or silver coin.
3. They are also called legal tenders as they cannot be refused by any citizen of the country for settlement of any kind of transaction.
4. Demand deposits like coins and notes are also legal tenders.

Which of these statements is/are incorrect?

(a) Only 1 (b) 1 and 2
(c) Only 4 (d) All of these

Ans. (c)

Exp. Only statement (4) is incorrect regarding currency notes and coins as demand deposits like coins and notes are not considered as legal tenders as they can be refused by anyone as a mode of payment. Currency notes and coins do not have any intrinsic value like gold and silver but they derive the value from the guarantee provided by the issuing authority of these items. Therefore, they are also called as flat money.

20 **Consider the following statements regarding the measures of money supply in India.** *(Chap 3, Class-XII, New NCERT)*

1. M1 refers to currency with the public + demand deposits with the banking system + other deposits with the RBI.
2. M4 refers to M3 + All deposits with the post office.

Which of the statements given above is/are correct?

(a) Only 1 (b) Only 2
(c) Both 1 and 2 (d) None of these

Ans. (c)

Exp. Both the statements (1) and (2) are correct.

Measures of Monetary and liquidity Aggregates.

M1 = Currency with public + Demand deposits with the banking system (current account, saving account) + Other deposits with RBI.

M2 = M1 + Savings deposits of post office savings banks.

M3 = M1 + Time deposits with the banking system.

M4 = M3 + All deposits with post office savings banks (excluding National Savings Certificates).

21 **Consider the following statements regarding terms of credit.** *(Chap 3, Class-XII, New NCERT)*

1. Interest rate, collateral and documentation requirement, and the mode of repayment together comprise, what is called the terms of credit.
2. Collateral is an asset that the borrower owns and uses this as a guarantee to a lender until the loan is repaid.
3. In case a borrower fails to repay the loan,the lender has the right to sell the asset or collateral to obtain payment only after the consent of the borrower.
4. Property such as land titles,deposits with banks, livestock are some common examples of collateral used for borrowing.

Which of the statements given above is/are incorrect?

(a) Only 1 (b) Only 2 and 3 (c) Only 3 (d) None of these

Ans. (c)

Exp. Only statement (3) is incorrect regarding the terms of credit as in case a borrower fails to repay the loan, the lender has the right to sell the asset or collateral to obtain payment without the consent of the borrower.

Collateral is an asset that the borrower owns and uses as a guarantee to lender until the loan is repaid. Property such as land, building, vehicle, livestock, deposits with banks, etc are the examples of collateral.

Interest rates, collateral and documentation requirement and the mode of repayment together comprise the terms of credit. The terms of credit may very depending on the nature of the lender and the borrower.

22 **Which of the following monetary instruments has the highest liquidity?** *(Chap 3, Class-XII, New NCERT)*

(a) Debenture (b) Credit Note
(c) Currency (d) Land or building

Ans. (c)

Exp. Among the given monetary instruments, currency has the highest liquidity.

It comes under the category of narrow money. Liquidity is the ability to convert an asset into cash and without losing money against the market price.

In other words, it is an asset that can easily be converted into cash in a short duration of time. Currency, saving accounts, money market instruments, marketable securities, etc., are some examples of liquid assets.

23 **Consider the following statements regarding bank in India.** *(Chap 3, Class-XII, New NCERT)*

1. The NARCL is a part of a new Bad bank.
2. India now has 12 PSBs instead of 27 from April 2020.
3. EASE 4.0 is a common reform agenda for PSBs.

Which of the statement(s) given above is/are correct?

(a) 1 and 2 (b) 1 and 3
(c) 2 and 3 (d) All of these

Ans. (d)

Exp. All the statements (1), (2) and (3) are correct regarding bank in India. The National Asset Reconstruction Company Limited (NARCL) is a part of a new Bad bank structure that was announced in the Budget 2021. NARCL has been incorporated under the Companies Act. Public Sector Banks (PSBs) will maintain 51% ownership in NARCL.

The Government of India has merged 10 state-owned banks (PSBs) into four. India now has only 12 PSBs in April 2019 instead of 27 (in 2017).

Union Finance Minister undertook the annual performance review of the Public Sector Banks (PSBs) and launched the EASE 4.0 or Enhanced Access and Service Excellence reform agenda.

EASE 4.0 is a common reform agenda for PSBs aimed at institutionalising clean and smart building.

24 **With reference to the Indian economy, consider the following statements.** *(Chap 7, Class-XII, New NCERT)*

1. 'Commercial Paper' is a short-term unsecured promissory note.
2. 'Certificate of Deposit' is a long-term instrument issued by the Reserve Bank of India to a corporation.
3. 'Call Money' is short-term finance used for interbank transactions.
4. 'Zero-Coupon Bonds' are the interest-bearing short-term bonds issued by the Scheduled Commercial Banks to corporations.

How many of the statements given above is/are correct?

(a) Only one
(b) Only two
(c) Only three
(d) All four

Ans. (d)

Exp. All four statements i.e., (1), (2), (3) and (4) are correct. 'Commercial Paper' is a short-term unsecured promissory note. It's typically used to finance short-term liabilities such as payroll, accounts payable and inventories.
'Certificate of Deposit' is a long-term instrument issued by the Reserve Bank of India to a corporation.
'Call Money' is short-term finance used for interbank transactions.Banks often use the interbank call money market to meet reserve requirements.
'Zero-Coupon Bonds' are the interest-bearing short-term bonds issued by the Scheduled Commercial Banks to corporations.

25 Consider the following statements. *(Chap 7, Class-XII, New NCERT)*

1. The committee on banking sector reforms was appointed by P. Chidamabaram in 1997.
2. It was headed by Narasimham.
3. It submitted its report to the then Finance Minister Yashwant Sinha in April 1998.

Which of the above statementis is/are correct?

(a) 1 and 2
(b) 2 and 3
(c) 1 and 3
(d) All of these

Ans. (d)

Exp. All of these statements are correct. The committee on banking sector reforms was appointed by P. Chidamabaram in 1997.It was headed by Narasimham. It submitted its report to the then Finance Minister Yashwant Sinha in April 1998.
Two Narasimham committees were set-up in the 1990s to satisfy the banking requirements. The Narasimham Committee 1 (Committee on the Financial System-CFS) was set-up by Manmohan Singh on 14th August, 1991. The Narasimham Committee 2 (Committee on Banking Sector Reforms) was set-up by P. Chidambaram in December 1997.

26 Consider the following statements. *(Chap 3, Class-XII, New NCERT) (IAS Pre 2023)*

1. Government Bond Market
2. Call Money Market
3. Treasury Bill Market
4. Stock Market

How many of the above markets is/are included in capital markets?

(a) Only one
(b) Only two
(c) Only three
(d) All four

Ans. (b)

Exp. Only two i.e., (1) and (4) market mentioned above are included in the capital markets that is Government Bond Market and the Stock Market. The other two, Call Money Market and Treasury Bill Market are part of the money market, as they deal with short-term financial instruments.
The capital market is where long-term assets, such as stocks and bonds, are traded. They money market is where short-term debt and lending takes place, usually for one year of less. The money market is less risky but alos less rewarding than the capital market, which is more volatile but potentially more profitable.

27 Which one of the following effects of creation of black money in India has been the main cause of worry to the Government of India ? *(Chap 3, Class-XII, New NCERT)* *(IAS Pre 2021)*

(a) Diversion of resources to the purchase of real estate and investment in luxury housing.
(b) Investment in unproductive activities and purchase of precious stones, jewellery, gold etc.
(c) Large donations to political parties and growth of regionalism.
(d) Loss of revenue to the state exchequer due to tax evasion.

Ans. (a)

Exp. Black money in India, is a term used to describe money that is illegitimately owned. Black money includes all funds earned through illegal activity and otherwise legal income that is not recorded for tax purposes.
Black money proceeds are usually received in cash from underground economic activity and as such, are not taxed. Such money needs to be retained as cash or in some other form which cannot be easily detected like precious metals and stones.
However, the biggest concern and worry of Government of India is loss of revenue to government due to tax evasion. Black money causes financial leakage, as unreported income that is not taxed causes the government to lose revenue. Black money can distort markets by artificially inflating prices and creating unfair competition.

28 Reserve Bank of India issues currency notes against which of the following? *(Chap 3, Class-XII, New NCERT)* *(MPPSC Pre 2022)*

(a) Gold
(b) Foreign Security
(c) Government of India Security
(d) All of these

Ans. (d)

Exp. The Reserve Bank of India (RBI) issues currency notes against assets such as **gold**, government securities and **foreign currency assets**. This is in accordance with Section 33 of the RBI Act, 1934.
The RBI holds gold reserves as a store of value and to back its currency. The amount of gold that the RBI holds is known as the gold backing. The RBI holds government securities as an investment. These securities are issued by the Government of India and are considered to be a safe investment. The RBI holds foreign currency assets to meet its foreign exchange obligations.

Chapter 09

Public Finance, Fiscal Policy and Budget

Public Finance Fiscal Policy And Budget

Public Finance

Introduction
- Studies revenue and expenditure of government of an economy
- Boundary in modern times is not limited to ways and means of government income

Fiscal Policy
- Refers to the use of government spending and tax policy
- Based on ideas from John Maynard Keynes

Features
- Measures by which government adjust its level of spending
- Feeds into economic trends and influence monetary policy

Financial Deficit

Amount by which a sum falls short of some reference amount

Types
- **Fiscal Deficit :** Gross fiscal Net fiscal Fiscal imbalancing
- **Revenue Deficit :** Variable includes only those transaction that affect current income
- **Capital Deficit :** Budget deficit Primary deficit Gross Primary
- **Monetary Losses :** Increment in net credit of RBI is monetary loss for the Central Government

Division

Public Expenditure

Revenue Expenditure
- Planned revenue expenditure
- Non planned revenue expenditure
- Capital expenditure

Public Income

Revenue Receipts
- In tax revenue
- Non tax revenue
- Taxable income
- Direct tax

Capital Receipts Capital gain are known as capital account

Government Budgeting

Introduction
- **The budget contains** Estimates of revenue and capital receipts;
- Estimates of expenditure; Policies of coming year

Historical Preview
- Derived from French word Bougette
- First used in France in 1803
- First budget of independence India in 1947

Objectives
- Rellocation of resources
- Reducing inequality
- Contributing to economic growth

Types
- Traditional
- Zero based
- Outcome
- Performance

Formation in India
- A quantitative expression of a plan for a defined period
- Financial Ministry sends circular forms to administrative affair for next financial year

Constitutional Fund of India

Consolidated Fund
- Most important of all government accounts
- It was constitutional under Article 266 (1)
- All Government expenditure is made from this fund expect exceptional items

Public Account
- Flows for those transaction where govt is merely acting as Banker
- Fund was constituted under Article 266 (2)

Contingency Fund
- Created as an imprest account to meet some urgent expenditure of government
- Fund at the disposal of the President

Goods and Services Tax GST

Introduction
- GST is a value added tax levied on most goods for domestic consumption
- Paid by customers, remitted to government by business selling the goods

Types
- **Central GST**
  - •A provision to impose tax on the supply of goods
  - •Excise duties, additional duty of custom duty, service tax, gratuity surcharges etc
- **State GST**
  - •Taxes imposed and collected by State Government
  - •State taxes, entry tax, purchase tax, entertainment taxes, etc
- **Integrated GST**
  - •Tax levied on international commodities and services
  - •Amount of taxes received under this is distribute to state
- **Union Territory GST**
  - •Provision under UTGST and tax system for UT
  - •UT have the provision to levy collected taxes by Central Government

Features
- Applicable on Supply side
- Destination based taxation
- Dual GST
- GST rates to be mutually decided
- Multiple rates

SOURCE *Old NCERT Class IX & X* (*The State and Economic Development*), ***New NCERT Class XII*** (*Government Budget and Economy*), ***Old NCERT Class XII*** (*Economy and Government Budget*)

1 Consider the following statements regarding the Government Budget.

(Chap 9, Class-XII, Tamil Nadu Board)

1. The Annual Financial Statement constitutes the main budget document of the government.
2. Statements that relate to the current financial year only are included in the revenue account.
3. The statements that concern the assets and liabilities of the government are included into the capital account.

How many statement(s) given above is/are correct?

(a) Only one (b) Only two
(c) All three (d) None of these

Ans. (c)

Exp. All the three statements i.e., (1), (2) and (3) are correct regarding the Government Budget.

Article 112 of the Indian Constitution entrust responsibility to the government to present before the Parliament a statement of expenditures of the government in respect of every financial year.

This Annual Financial Statement constitutes the main budget document of the government, It is further divided into two accounts-revenue and capital account.

The statements that relate to the current financial year, only are included in revenue account and those financial statements that concern with the assets and liabilities of the government are included into capital account.

2 Which of the following is/are the functions of the Government Budget in India?

(Chap 5, Class-XII, New NCERT)

1. Resource allocation
2. Redistribution of funds to various government's programme
3. Inflation targeting

Select the correct answer using the codes given below.

(a) 1 and 2
(b) Only 2
(c) 1 and 3
(d) All of these

Ans. (a)

Exp. The functions of the Government Budget in India are to redistribution of funds to various government programme and allocation of resources.

While inflation targeting is not a part of Government Budget. It is the task of Monetary Policy Committee to manage inflation within country.

3 Consider the following Assertion (A) and Reason (R) and choose the correct code.

(Chap 5, Class-XII, New NCERT)

Assertion (A) The government can change the distribution of income and bring about a distribution that is considered 'fair' by society.

Reason (R) The government sector affects the personal disposable income of households by making transfers and collecting taxes.

Codes

(a) Both A and R are true and R is the correct explanation of A.
(b) Both A and R are true, but R is not the correct explanation of A.
(c) A is true, but R is false.
(d) A is false, but R is true.

Ans. (a)

Exp. Both Assertion (A) and Reason (R) are true and Reason (R) is the correct explanation of Assertion (A).
Government through its redistribution mechanisms (such as taxes, subsidies, scholarships, etc) can change the distribution of income and bring about a distribution that is considered 'fair' by the society. It is one of the most important tool for achieving the goal of inclusive development. Also through transfers (such as scholarship, grant, subsidies, etc.) and collecting taxes, the government affects the personal disposable income of households.

4 Consider the following statements regarding Gender Budgeting in India. *(Chap 5, Class-XII, New NCERT)*

1. It was first introduced in Union Budget 2005-2006.
2. It allows policymakers to allocate funds and direct expenditure keeping in mind the requirement of female in India.

Which of the statements given above is/are correct?

(a) Only 1 (b) Only 2
(c) Both 1 and 2 (d) Neither 1 nor 2

Ans. (c)

Exp. Both statements (1) and (2) are correct regarding Gender Budgeting in India. It was first time introduced in the Union Budget 2005-2006. It allows policymakers to allocate funds and direct expenditure keeping in mind the requirement of female in India. It means preparing budgets or analysing them from a gender perspective.

It aims at dealing with budgetary gender inequality issues, including gender hierarchies and the discrepancies between women's and men's salaries.

5 Consider the following Assertion (A) and Reason (R) and choose the correct code.

(Chap 5, Class-IX & X, Old NCERT)

Assertion (A) Revenue receipts are termed as non-redeemable.

Reason (R) Revenue receipts are those receipts that do not lead to a claim on the government.

Codes

(a) Both A and R are true and R is the correct explanation of A.
(b) Both A and R are true, but R is not the correct explanation of A.
(c) A is true, but R is false.
(d) A is false, but R is true.

Ans. (a)

Exp. Both Assertion (A) and Reason (R) are true and Reason (R) is the correct explanation of Assertion (A).

Revenue receipts are termed as non-redeemable. They are always recurring in nature and do not have a direct impact on the assets and liabilities of the government.

Also these receipts do not lead to a claim on the government. Tax revenues are an important component of revenue receipts.

6 Consider the following statements about revenue receipts. *(Chap 5, Class-XII, New NCERT)*

1. They are divided into tax and non-tax revenues.
2. Tax revenues have been divided into direct taxes and indirect taxes like excise taxes, customs duties and GST.

Which of the statement(s) given above is/are correct?

(a) Only 1 (b) Only 2
(c) Both 1 and 2 (d) Neither 1 nor 2

Ans. (c)

Exp. Both the statements (1) and (2) are correct regarding revenue receipts.

Those receipts that do not lead to claim on the government and are recurring in nature are termed as revenue receipts. They are divided into tax and non-tax revenues.

Tax revenue have been further divided into direct taxes like income tax, corporation tax and indirect taxes like excise taxes, custom duties and service tax.

Non-tax revenue constitutes dividends and profits on investment made by government, fees and other receipts rendered by the government.

7 Consider the following statements regarding non-debt creating capital receipts. *(Chap 5, Class-XII, New NCERT)*

1. Non-debt creating capital receipts are those receipts which are not borrowings and, therefore, do not give rise to debt.
2. Recovery of loans and the proceeds from the sale of PSUs are examples of non-debt creating capital receipts.

Which of the statements given above is/are incorrect?

(a) Only 1 (b) Only 2
(c) Both 1 and 2 (d) Neither 1 nor 2

Ans. (d)

Exp. Neither statement (1) nor (2) is incorrect regarding non-debt creating capital receipts.

All those receipts of the government which create liability or reduce financial assets are termed as capital receipts. They may or may not create debts. Non-debt creating capital receipts are those receipts which are not borrowings and therefore, do not give rise to debt. The recovery of loans and the proceeds from the sale of Public Sector Undertaking (PSUs) are some of the examples of non-debt creating capital receipts. It is useful in calculating the fiscal deficit.

8 Which of the following is/are the example of Non-tax revenue? *(Chap 5, Class-XII, New NCERT)*

1. Dividends 2. Disinvestment 3. Fees
4. Excise duty 5. Estate duty

Select the correct answer using the codes given below.

(a) 1, 2 and 4 (b) 1, 2 and 3 (c) 2, 3 and 5 (d) 3, 4 and 5

Ans. (b)

Exp. Dividends, disinvestment and fees are examples of Non-tax revenue. The incomes accuring to government from sources other than taxes are non-tax revenues. The following are some of the most important non-tax revenue sources: interest, disinvestment, profits dividends, fees, fines, penalties and grants.

9 Consider the following statements regarding paper tax. *(Chap 5, Class-XII, New NCERT)*

1. It carry their significance only on paper and have no significance in terms of revenue yield.
2. Entertainment tax is the part of paper tax.

Which of the statements given above is/are correct?

(a) Only 1 (b) Only 2
(c) Both 1 and 2 (d) Neither 1 nor 2

Ans. (a)

Exp. Only statement (1) is correct with reference to paper tax. It carry their significance only on paper and have no significance in terms of revenue yield. For instance : wealth tax and gift tax.

Statement (2) is incorrect. Entertainment tax is not a paper tax rather it comes under the ambit of GST.

10 Consider the following statements with respect to Revenue expenditure. *(Chap 5, Class-XII, New NCERT)*

1. It is expenditure incurred for purposes other than the creation of physical or financial assets of Central Government.
2. It relates to the expenses incurred for the normal functioning of the government departments and various services, interest payment on debt incurred by government and grant given to State Government.

Which of the statements given above is/are correct?

(a) Only 1 (b) Only 2
(c) Both 1 and 2 (d) Neither 1 nor 2

Ans. (c)

Exp. Both statements (1) and (2) are correct regarding Revenue expenditure. It refers to any money spent by a business that covers short-term expenses. This means the money is used for expenses that are used within one year. Revenue expenditure does not include expenditure for the creation of physical or financial assets of Central Government.

Capital expenditure includes creation of physical and financial assets. Revenue expenditure includes expenses of various departments, interest payment and grants given to state by Central Government.

11 One of the most significant Fiscal Policy objectives in India is to bring the revenue expenditures and receipts to the same level. Which of the following steps will help to achieve that objective?
(Chap 5, Class-XII, New NCERT)

1. The efforts to raise the total profits for public sector units.
2. The efforts to improve the revenues from tax collection.
3. The efforts to slow the growth rate for expenditures in the country.

Which of the statements given above is/are correct?

(a) 1 and 2 (b) Only 2
(c) 2 and 3 (d) All of these

Ans. (d)

Exp. All of the given statements are correct.

All the given steps will help to achieve that objective. Fiscal Policy is an estimate of taxation and government expending that impacts the economy. The key objectives of Fiscal Policy are economic stability, price stability, full employment, optimum allocation of resources, accelerating the rate of economical development, capital formation and growth.

12 Which of the following items is classified as a capital receipt in the budget for the Government of India?
(Chap 5, Class-XII, New NCERT)

1. The borrowing made by the government from the public.
2. The receipts from the collection of income tax.
3. The dividends and profits received from the public sector units.

How many of the above statement(s) is/are incorrect?

(a) Only one
(b) Only two
(c) All three
(d) None of the above

Ans. (b)

Exp. Only two statements i.e., (2) and (3) are incorrect because collection of income tax, dividends and profits received from the public units are part of revenue receipt. Recovery of loans given by the centre to states and others is also included in capital receipts. The capital receipt has a nature of non-recurrence.

13 Consider the following statements in respect of the budget deficit. *(Chap 5, Class-XII, New NCERT)*

1. Budget deficit is defined when excess of total expenditure over the total receipts.
2. Budget deficit does not consider foreign borrowings.

How many of the above statement(s) is/are incorrect?

(a) Only 1 (b) Only 2
(c) Both 1 and 2 (d) Neither 1 nor 2

Ans. (b)

Exp. Statement (2) is incorrect because fiscal deficit is the difference between the total income of the government (total taxes and non-debt capital receipts) and its total expenditure. While calculating the total revenue, borrowings are not included.

14 Expenditure of the government which result in the creation of physical or financial assets or reduction in financial liabilities is known as which of the following? *(Chap 5, Class-XII, New NCERT)*

(a) Plan Expenditure (b) Non-Plan Expenditure
(c) Capital Expenditure (d) Revenue Expenditure

Ans. (c)

Exp. Expenditure of the government which result in the creation of physical or financial assets or reduction in financial liabilities is known as Capital Expenditure.

It includes expenditure on the acquisition of land, building, machinery, investment in shares, and loans and advances by the Central Government to State and Union Territory governments, Public Sector Undertakings (PSUs) and other parties.

15 Which of the following expenditures is not an example of capital expenditure?
(Chap 5, Class-XII, New NCERT)

1. Acquisition of land 2. Investment in shares
3. Loans and advances 4. Grant-in-Aid
5. Direct and indirect taxes

Select the correct answer using the codes given below.

(a) 1 and 2 (b) 3 and 4 (c) 2 and 3 (d) 4 and 5

Ans. (d)

Exp. Grant-in-aid and direct and indirect taxes are not part of capital expenditure. These are classified under revenue expenditure of government. Capital expenditure are incurred for purpose of creation of physical and financial assets. Acquisition of land, investment in share and loans and advances are part of capital expenditure.

16 Which of the following statements is incorrect?
(Chap 5, Class-XII, New NCERT)

(a) Capital expenditure includes interest payments on debt incurred by the government and grants given to State Governments and other parties.
(b) Budget documents classify total expenditure into plan and non-plan expenditure.
(c) Plan revenue expenditure relates to central plans and central assistance for state and Union Territory plans.
(d) Non-plan expenditure covers a vast range of general, economic and social services of the government.

Ans. (a)

Exp. Statement (a) is incorrect as interest payments on debt incurred by the government and grants given to State Governments and other parties are included in revenue expenditure not in capital expenditure.

It is usually incurred for purposes other than the creation of physical or financial assets of the government.

17 Consider the following statements about Budgetary Deficits. *(Chap 5, Class-XII, New NCERT)*

1. The revenue deficit refers to the excess of government's revenue expenditure over revenue receipts.
2. Primary deficit is the difference between the government's total expenditure and its total receipts excluding borrowing.

Which of the statement(s) given above is/are incorrect?

(a) Only 1 (b) Only 2
(c) Both 1 and 2 (d) Neither 1 nor 2

Ans. (b)

Exp. Statement (2) is incorrect regarding Budgetary Deficits. It is a financial condition wherein the expenditure of the government exceeds its revenue. Primary deficit is the fiscal deficit minus (deduction) the interest payment and helps in focussing the present fiscal imbalances of the government.

18 Consider the following statements about fiscal deficit. *(Chap 5, Class-XII, New NCERT)*

1. It is the difference between the government's total expenditure and its total receipts excluding borrowing.
2. It indicates the total borrowing requirements of the government from all sources.
3. It does not cover revenue receipt of government.

How many of the above statements is/are correct?

(a) Only one (b) Only two
(c) All three (d) None of these

Ans. (b)

Exp. Only two statements i.e., (1) and (2) are correct regarding to fiscal deficit of government.

Fiscal deficit is the difference between government's total expenditure and its total revenue (excluding borrowing). It is an indicator of the extent to which the government must borrow in order to finance its operations and is expressed as percentage of the country's GDP. It does cover both revenue and capital receipts of the government.

19 Which of the following statements is incorrect regarding the features of the Fiscal Responsibility and Budget Management (FRBM) Act? *(Chap 5, Class-XII, New NCERT)*

1. The Act mandates the Central Government to take appropriate measures to reduce revenue deficit to not more than 3% of GDP and to eliminate the fiscal deficit.
2. The actual deficits may exceed the targets specified only on grounds of national security or natural calamity.
3. The Reserve Bank of India must not subscribe to the primary issues of Central Government securities from the year 2006-2007.
4. Quarterly review of the trends in receipts and expenditure in relation to the budget be placed before both the Houses of Parliament.

Select the correct answer using the codes given below.

(a) 1, 2 and 3 (b) Only 2 (c) 2, 3 and 4 (d) All of these

Ans. (b)

Exp. Statement (2) is incorrect because the FRBM Act does allow for deviations from the specified targets, but not solely on grounds of national security or natural calamity. The Act provides for an 'escape clause' that permits deviations due to exceptional circumstances, including national security, war and calamities.

20 Alongwith the budget, which of the following policy statements are mandated by the Fiscal Responsibility and Budget Management (FRBM) Act, 2003? *(Chap 5, Class-XII, New NCERT)*

1. Medium-term Fiscal Policy Statement
2. The Fiscal Policy Strategy Statement
3. The Macroeconomic Framework Statement
4. Short-term Fiscal Policy Statement

Codes

(a) 1 and 4 (b) 1, 2 and 3
(c) 1 and 2 (d) 1, 2, 3 and 4

Ans. (b)

Exp. The following policies (1), (2) and (3) are mandated by the Fiscal Responsibility and Budget Management (FRBM) Act, 2003.

It mandated the government to place in Parliament a medium term fiscal policy statement, the fiscal policy strategy statement and macroeconomic framework statement along with the budget in Parliament.

While it helps in following a prudent fiscal policy and ensuring inter-generational equity and long-term macroeconomic stability by achieving sufficient revenue surplus.

21 Alongwith the Budget, the Finance Minister also places other documents before the Parliament which includes 'The Macroeconomic Framework Statement'. The aforesaid document is presented because this is mandated by *(Chap 5, Class-XII, New NCERT) (IAS Pre 2020)*

(a) Long standing Parliament convention.
(b) Article 112 and Article 110(1) of the Constitution of India.
(c) Article 113 of the Constitution of India.
(d) Provisions of the Fiscal Responsibility and Budget Management Act, 2003.

Ans. (d)

Exp. Financial Responsibility and Budget Management Act, 2003 mandated to place 'The Macroeconomic Framework Statement' along with Budget before the Parliament.

This Act aims towards ensuring long-term macroeconomic stability and inter-generational equity by creating statutory basis for effective debt management. It also contains legislative provisions directing the government to reduce Fiscal and Revenue Deficit and to follow a policy of fiscal prudence.

22 Consider the following statements with respect to the Goods and Services Tax (GST).

(Chap 5, Class-XII, New NCERT)

1. Goods and Services Tax (GST) is the single comprehensive indirect tax, operational from 1st July, 2017, on supply of goods and services from the manufacturer to the consumer.
2. It is a source based consumption tax with the facility of Input Tax Credit in the supply chain.

Which of the statement(s) given above is/are incorrect?

(a) Only 1
(b) Only 2
(c) Both 1 and 2
(d) Neither 1 nor 2

Ans. (b)

Exp. Statement (2) is incorrect regarding GST as it is a destination based (not source based) consumption tax with the facility of Input Tax Credit in the supply chain. Goods and Services Tax (GST) is a Value Added Tax levied on most goods and services sold for domestic consumption. GST is paid by consumers, but it is remitted to the government by the businesses selling the goods and services.

23 What is/are the most likely advantages of implementing 'Goods and Services Tax (GST)'?

(Chap 5, Class-XII, New NCERT), (IAS Pre 2017)

1. It will replace multiple taxes collected by multiple authorities and will thus create a single market in India.
2. It will drastically reduce the 'Current Account Deficit' of India and will enable it to increase its foreign exchange reserves.
3. It will enormously increase the growth and size of economy of India and will enable it to overtake China in the near future.

Select the correct answer using the codes given below.

(a) Only 1 (b) 2 and 3 (c) 1 and 3 (d) 1, 2 and 3

Ans. (a)

Exp. Statement (1) is correct as GST will replace multiple taxes collected by multiple authorities and will thus create a single market in India.

Statements (2) and (3) are incorrect as GST is unlikely to drastically reduce Current Account Deficit because crude oil report and OPEC cartel that manipulates its prices.

GST is unlikely to enormously increase the growth and size of economy because the IMF projection is 1-1.5% addition in growth rate. We can't overtake China in near future, because it will require currency undervaluation and labour exploitation.

24 Which among the following taxes has not been subsumed under the GST?

(Chap 5, Class-XII, New NCERT)

1. Central sales tax 2. Luxury tax 3. Custom tax

Codes

(a) 1 and 2
(b) 2 and 3
(c) Only 3
(d) None of these

Ans. (c)

Exp. Only statement (3) is correct with regarding to GST. The taxes subsumed in GST include Central Excise Duty, Service Tax, VAT and Several other taxes. However, direct taxes such as Income tax, Customs duty on imports and taxes on petroleum products are not subsumed under the GST.

25 Which of the following statements is not one of the advantages of the GST? *(Chap 5, Class-XII, New NCERT)*

(a) GST has simplified the multiplicity of taxes on goods and services.
(b) It has facilitated the freedom of movement of goods and services and created a common market in the country.
(c) It is aimed at increasing the cascading effect of various taxes on consumers.
(d) It has also reduced the overall cost of production, which will make Indian products/services more competitive in the domestic and international markets.

Ans. (c)

Exp. Statement (c) is not one of the advantages of GST as it is aimed at eliminating the cascading (not increasing) effect of various taxes on consumers. GST, which subsumed almost all domestic indirect taxes under one head, is perhaps the biggest tax reform in the history of independent India. It was launched in operation on the midnight of 1st July, 2017.

26 Consider the following statements with respect to the Goods and Services Tax.

(Chap 5, Class-XII, New NCERT)

1. State Governments will continue to levy VAT on alcoholic liquor for human consumption.
2. Under GST, there are 5 standard rates applied i.e. 0%, 5%, 12%,18% and 28% on supply of all goods or services across the country.

Which of the statement(s) given above is/are correct?

(a) Only 1
(b) Only 2
(c) Both 1 and 2
(d) Neither 1 nor 2

Ans. (c)

Exp. Both the statements (1) and (2) are correct with respect to the GST, as it allows State Governments to levy VAT (Value Added Tax) on alcoholic liquor for human consumption. Petroleum products also has been kept out from the ambit of GST. As of December 2021, there are 5 GST rates slab operational in the country, i.e 0%, 5%, 12%, 18% and 28% on supply of all goods and services across the country.

Chapter 10

Foreign Trade and Balance of Payment

Foreign Trade and Balance of Payment

Foreign Trade/Foreign Trade Policy (FTP)

Foreign Trade

- The exchange of capital goods and services across international border territories
- All about imports and exports

Types

- **Visible trade** trade in goods means, physical things
- **Invisible trade** trade like tourism and banking

Components

- **Export** a process whereby goods produced in one country and shipped from another country e.g. Handicraft, ore and minerals
- **Import** a process where goods services are bought from other country e.g. Edible oil, Petroleum

Foreign Trade Policy (FTP)

Formulation in India

- Formulated by Ministry of Commerce and industry
- India uses FTP to attain short term goals

New FTP (2021-26)

- Goal is to make India a 5 trillion USD economy; It aims to boost exports
- Came into effect from 1st April, 2021

Balance of Payment (BOP)

Components

Current Account

Balance

- Balance of trade or trade balance
- Balances on invisibles

Deficit

- Measured as percentage of GDP
- A high deficit leads to higher CAD and *vice-versa*

Capital Account

Components

- Borrowing and lendings from foreign country
- Investment to and from the foreign countries
- Foreign Direct Investment

Balance

- Capital account is in balance when capital inflows
- Deficit in capital account arises when capital inflows are lesser than outflows

Present Status in India (BOP)

- Irreversible Trade Deficit – Rise in Imports

Currency Convertibility

Current

- Refers to the freedom in payments
- India was obliged to do as per Article 8 of (IMF)
- Limits have been imposed on convertibility

Capital

- CAD should be brought down to manageable limits to be reduced to 20% from 25% of export earnings

Foreign Exchange Market

Determination of the Exchange Rate

Foreign Exchange Rate

- Also called forex rate
- Reduce the foreigner's cost while purchasing in India

Fixed Exchange Rate

- Achieved by linking the domestic currency to the value of Gold
- Government has responsible to intervene and maintain the exchange rate

Floating Exchange Rate

- Neither the government nor the Central Bank intervenes and the market functions freely
- It ensures that a country access easy loans from IMF

Managed Floating Exchange Rate

- Adjusted Peg System
- Crawling Peg System
- Clean Floating – Dirty Floating

Exchange Rate Management in India

- Per value system till 1971
- Pegged Regime
- Partial Convertibility after 1991
- Market based Exchange Rate Regime since 1993

SOURCE **Old NCERT Class IX & X** *(Towards Economic Development)*, **New NCERT Class X** *(Globalisation and the Indian Economy)*, **New NCERT Class X** *(Indian Economy on the Eve of Independence)*, **New NCERT Class XI** *(Indian Economy 1950-1990)*, **New NCERT Class XII** *(Open Economy : Macroeconomics)*, **Old NCERT Class XII** *(Balance of Payment)*, **Old NCERT Class XII** *(Foreign Exchange Rates : Meaning and Assessment)*

1 **With reference to international trade, consider the following statements.** *(Chap 7, Class-XII, Tamil Nadu Board)*

1. The classical theory explains the phenomenon of international trade on the basis of labour theory of value.
2. The modern theory explains the phenomenon of international trade on the basis of general theory of value.

Which of the statements given above is/are correct?

(a) Only 1 (b) Only 2
(c) Both 1 and 2 (d) Neither 1 nor 2

Ans. (c)

Exp. Both statements (1) and (2) are correct with reference to international trade. The classical theory explains the phenomenon of international trade on the basis of labour theory of value. It presents a one factor (labour) model.

The modern theory explains the phenomenon of international trade on the basis of general theory of value. It presents a multi-factor (labour and capital) model.

3 **Which of the following statements is/are correct regarding foreign trade?** *(Chap 4, Class-IX & X, Old NCERT)*

(a) The Balance of Trade (BoT) is the difference between the monetary value of a nation's exports and imports of goods and services in a particular year.
(b) If exports are more than imports, then the balance of trade is positive.
(c) In case of imports higher than exports, there is decline in foreign exchange reserves.
(d) All of the above

Ans. (d)

Exp. All the given statements i.e., (a), (b) and (c) are correct regarding the foreign trade. Balance of Trade (BoT) is the difference between the value of exports and the value of imports of goods of a country in a given period of time. It is also known as Trade Balance. With reference to balance sheet, it can be positive, negative or balanced. When exports and imports are equal, it is considered balanced. When exports are greater than imports, the Balance of trade is positive and it is negative when imports surpass the exports. In case, imports are higher than exports, there is decline in foreign exchange reserve whereas higher exports than imports leads to increase in foreign exchange reserves.

2 **With reference to open trade, consider the following statements.** *(Chap 4, Class-X, New NCERT)*

1. Choice of goods in the markets rises.
2. Prices of the same goods in the two markets tend to become equal.
3. The cost differential of producing a commodity discourages trade between countries.

How many statements given above is/are incorrect?

(a) Only one (b) Only two
(c) All three (d) None of these

Ans. (a)

Exp. Only one statement i.e., (3) is incorrect with reference to open trade as the reason behind increase in trade between countries is the cost differential of producing a commodity. It refers to export of goods which are cost effective to produce and import of goods which are expensive to produce in the country but cheap in other countries. Factors of production such as land, labour, resources etc. affect the cost of production.

4 **Identify the incorrect statement regarding the features of Special Economic Zone (SEZ).** *(Chap 4, Class-X, New NCERT)*

(a) To attract foreign companies to invest in India, Industrial zones called Special Economic Zones (SEZs), are being set up.
(b) Companies who set up production units in the SEZs do not have to pay taxes for an initial period of five years.
(c) Instead of hiring workers on a part time basis, companies hire workers 'flexibly' for longer periods.
(d) Government has also allowed flexibility in the labour laws to attract foreign investment.

Ans. (c)

Exp. Statement (c) is incorrect regarding Special Economic Zone (SEZ) as in this zone companies hire workers for short periods when there is intense pressure of work. Special Economic Zone (SEZ) are one of the innovative steps by government to attract foreign companies to invest in India. Special Economic Zone is an area which is set up to incentivise businesses. SEZs offer competitive infrastructure, duty free exports, tax incentives and other measures designed to make production cheaper and exports more competitive.

5 **Consider the following statements regarding Foreign Trade of India in the British era.** *(Chap 1, Class-XI, New NCERT)*

1. More than half of India's foreign trade was restricted to Britain while the rest was allowed with a few other countries like China, Ceylon (Sri Lanka) and Persia (Iran).
2. India's economy under the British colonial rule remained fundamentally service oriented.

Which of the statements given above is/are correct?

(a) Only 1 (b) Only 2
(c) Both 1 and 2 (d) Neither 1 nor 2

Ans. (a)

Exp. Statement (1) is correct regarding Foreign Trade of India in the British era.

Restrictive policies of commodity production, trade and tariff pursued by the colonial government adversely affected the structure, composition and volume of India's Foreign Trade.

As a result, India became exporter of primary goods and importer of finished goods; further more than half of India's foreign trade was restricted to Britain while the rest was allowed with a few other countries like China, Ceylon (Sri Lanka) and Persia (Iran).

Statement (2) is incorrect as India's economy under the British colonial rule remained fundamentally agrarian (not service oriented). About 85% of the country's population lived mostly in villages and derived livelihood directly or indirectly from agriculture.

6 Which one of the following measures is not likely to aid in improving India's Balance of Payment position? *(Chap 10, Class-XII, New NCERT) (BPSC Pre 2018)*

(a) Promotion of Import Substitution Policy
(b) Devaluation of Rupee
(c) Imposition of Higher Tariff on Imports
(d) Levying of Higher Duties on Exports

Ans. (d)

Exp. Levying of Higher Duties on Exports is not likely to aid in improving India's Balance of Payment position. It will make exports costlier, thereby decreasing competitiveness of India's trade with the rest of the world.

7 Consider the following statements. *(Chap 2, Class-XI, New NCERT)*

1. Import substitution aimed at replacing or substituting exports with domestic production.
2. Protection from imports took two forms-tariffs and quotas.

Which of the statements given above is/are incorrect?

(a) Only 1 (b) Only 2
(c) Both 1 and 2 (d) Neither 1 nor 2

Ans. (a)

Exp. Statement (1) is incorrect as import substitution followed by India after independence aimed at replacing or substituting imports with domestic production. It helps in protecting the domestic firms from foreign competition.

8 With reference to 'Balance of Payment', consider the following statements. *(Chap 7, Class-XII, Tamil Nadu Board)*

1. It records transactions in goods and services only.
2. Transfer payments are receipts which the resident of a country receives for free.
3. Official reserve assets account doesn't form one of the components of BOPs.

How many statements given above are incorrect?

(a) Only one (b) Only two
(c) All three (d) None of these

Ans. (b)

Exp. Only two statements i.e. (1) and (3) are incorrect regarding Balance of Payment as it records the transaction of goods, services and assets between residents of a country with the rest of the world for a specified time period typically a year.

The official reserve assets account form one of the components of BoP's.

9 The Balance of Payment of an economy is a systematic record of which of the following? *(Chap 10, Class-XII, Old NCERT) (IAS Pre 2012)*

(a) All economic transactions between residents of a country and the rest of the world in a given period.
(b) Movement of capital from one country to another.
(c) Economic transaction between the governments of two countries.
(d) Capital movements from one country to another.

Ans. (a)

Exp. The Balance of Payment of an economy is a systematic record of all economic transactions (goods, services and assets) between residents of a country and the rest of the world in a given period.

There are three main accounts in the Balance of Payment (BoP) i.e., the current account, the capital account and the financial account. The current account records exports and imports in goods and services and transfer payments. The capital account records all international purchases and sales of assets such as money, stocks, bonds, etc.

10 Which of the following forms part of the Current Account of the Balance of Payment? *(Chap 10, Class-XII, Old NCERT) (IAS Pre 2014)*

1. Trade Balance 2. Foreign Asset
3. Invisibles 4. Special Drawing Rights

Select the correct answer using the codes given below.

(a) 1, 2 and 4 (b) 1 and 3 (c) 2 and 4 (d) 1, 2, 3 and 4

Ans. (b)

Exp. Trade balance and invisibles forms the part of the Current Account of the Balance of Payment. In this account, trade in services denoted as invisible trade because they are not seen to cross national borders.

The current account of the Balance of Payments includes a country's key activity, such as capital markets and services. The four major components of a current account are goods, services, income and current transfers.

11 Balance of Payments is an accounting statement that records the economic transactions between *(Chap 6, Class-XII, New NCERT)*

(a) residents of a country and non-resident individuals.
(b) residents of a country and rest of the world.
(c) non-residents and rest of the world.
(d) None of the above

Ans. (b)

Exp. The Balance of Payments is an accounting statement that records the economic transactions between residents of a country and rest of the world because it is the difference between all money flowing into the country in a particular period of time and the outflow of money to the rest of the world.

The Balance of Payments consists of three main components i.e., current account, capital account and financial account.

12 With reference to Balance of Payment (BoP), consider the following statements. *(Chap 7, Class-XII, Tamil Nadu Board)*

1. When the receipts exceed payments, the BoP is said to be unfavourable.
2. Difference in the elasticities of demand between two countries creates cyclical disequilibrium of Balance of Payment.
3. Low developed countries suffer from adverse BoP as their import intensity is very high.

How many statements given above is/are correct?

(a) Only one (b) Only two
(c) All three (d) None of these

Ans. (b)

Exp. Only two statements i.e., (2) and (3) are correct with reference to Balance of Payment (BoP). The difference in elasticities of demand between two countries creates cyclical disequilibrium. Cyclical equilibrium also occurs when countries may be passing through different phases of the business cycle.

Low development countries suffer from adverse BoP, due to low export potential and when the import intensity is high.

Statement (1) is incorrect. Balance of Payments is unfavourable when the payments (debit) of the country is more than its receipts (credit). Meanwhile, when the receipts (credit) are more than the payments (debit) the BoP is said to be favourable.

13 With reference to BoP, consider the following statements. *(Chap 6, Class-XII, New NCERT)*

1. Balance of current account deals with debts and claims of a country.
2. Accommodating items is the economic transactions which are undertaken to make equilibrium in balance of payment.

Which of the statements given above is/are correct?

(a) Only 1
(b) Only 2
(c) Both 1 and 2
(d) Neither 1 nor 2

Ans. (b)

Exp. Only statement (2) is correct with reference to BoP. Accommodating items is the economic transactions which are undertaken to make equilibrium in balance of payment.

Accommodating transactions refer to deliberate transactions undertaken by the Central Bank or Government to maintain the balance of payments equilibrium, such as buying or selling foreign currency reserves or adjusting interest rates

Statement (1) is incorrect. The current account deals with the inflow and outflow of money within a given year for a particular country.

14 Balance of Trade is *(Chap 4, Class-IX & X, Old NCERT)*

(a) difference between export and import of goods.
(b) sum total of export and import of goods.
(c) difference between export and import of services.
(d) sum total of export and import services.

Ans. (a)

Exp. The Balance of Trade is the difference between the value of a country's exports and the value of its imports. Formula for Balance of Trade is

Balance of Trade = Country's Exports − Country's Imports

15 Which of the following constitute Capital Account? *(Chap 10, Class-XII, Old NCERT) (IAS Pre 2013)*

1. Foreign Loans 2. Foreign Direct Investment
3. Private Remittances 4. Portfolio Investment

Select the correct answer using the codes given below.

(a) 1, 2 and 3 (b) 1, 2 and 4 (c) 2, 3 and 4 (d) 1, 3 and 4

Ans. (b)

Exp. Foreign Loans, Foreign Direct Investment and Portfolio Investment constitute Capital Account.

It records all international purchases and sales of assets such as currency, stocks, bonds, etc.

The Capital account balance of a country is equal to capital flows from the rest of the world, minus capital flows to the rest of the world. Private remittances are constituent of current account which is sum of the balance of merchandise trade, services and net transfers received from rest of the world.

16 Consider the following statements. *(Chap 10, Class-XII, New NCERT)*

1. According to new classification of BoP accounts, the transactions are divided into three accounts.
2. Current Account deficit is measured as a percentage of GDP.
3. Capital Account records all international transactions of assets.

Which of the statements given above is/are correct?

(a) 1, 2 and 3 (b) 2 and 3 (c) 1 and 3 (d) 1 and 2

Ans. (a)

Exp. All the three statements i.e., (1), (2) and (3) are correct. RBI made changes in the structure of Balance of Payments (BoP) accounts. According to the new classification, the transactions are divided into three accounts i.e., Current account, Financial Account and Capital account. All the transactions arising on account of trade in financial assets such as bonds and equity shares are now placed in the financial accounts.

There is a deficit in current account if the value of the goods and services imported exceeds, the value of those exported. Current Account Deficit is measured as a percentage of GDP. Capital Account records all international transactions of assets. Purchase of assets is a debit item on capital account. The Sale of assets is a credit items on the capital account.

17 **With reference to the Indian economy, consider the following statements.**
(Chap 6, Class-XII, New NCERT), (IAS Pre 2022)

1. An increase in Nominal Effective Exchange Rate (NEER) indicates the appreciation of rupee.
2. An increase in the Real Effective Exchange Rate (REER) indicates an improvement in trade competitiveness.
3. An increasing trend in domestic inflation relative to inflation in other countries is likely to cause an increasing divergence between NEER and REER.

Which of the statements given above are correct?

(a) 1 and 2 (b) 2 and 3
(c) 1 and 3 (d) 1, 2 and 3

Ans. *(c)*

Exp. Both statements (1) and (3) are correct with reference to the exchange rate.

The Nominal Effective Exchange Rate (NEER) is an unadjusted weighted average rate at which one country's currency exchanges for a basket of multiple foreign currencies. The nominal exchange rate is the amount of domestic currency needed to purchase foreign currency. It is a measure of the value of a currency against a weighted average of several foreign currencies. An increase in NEER indicates an appreciation of the rupee. The NEER is the weighted geometric average of the bilateral nominal exchange rates of the home currency in terms of foreign currencies. The REER is the weighted average of NEER adjusted by the ratio of domestic prices to foreign prices.

An increasing trend in domestic inflation relative to inflation in other countries creates a divergence in NEER and REER.

18 **Which of the following is/are included in the Foreign Exchange Reserves?**
(Chap 10, Class-XII, Old NCERT)

1. Foreign Currency
2. Gold
3. Special Drawing Rights
4. Foreign Securities

Select the correct answer using the codes given below.

(a) 1, 2, 3 and 4 (b) 1 and 3
(c) 2 and 4 (d) 1, 3 and 4

Ans. *(a)*

Exp. Foreign Currency, Gold, Special Drawing Rights (SDR) and Foreign Securities are included in the Foreign Exchange Reserves of the country.

These assets are held by nation's Central Bank or monetary authority (RBI in case of India).

Special drawing rights are supplementary foreign currency assets maintained by IMF, a country can borrow it from IMF during a balance of payment crisis. It is helpful in meeting any adverse scenario in case of Balance of Payment crisis and limiting external vulnerability.

19 **Consider the following statements about the Foreign Exchange Rate.** *(Chap 6, Class-XII, New NCERT)*

1. Foreign Exchange Rate is the price of one currency in terms of another.
2. It links the currencies of different countries and enables comparison of international costs and prices.

Which of the statement(s) given above is/are correct?

(a) Only 1 (b) Only 2
(c) Both 1 and 2 (d) Neither 1 nor 2

Ans. *(c)*

Exp. Both statements (1) and (2) are correct regarding Foreign Exchange Rate. The price of one currency in terms of the other is known as the exchange rate. It can also be defined as the amount of domestic currency required to buy one unit of foreign currency. In foreign exchange market, national currencies are traded for one another.

Foreign exchange market links the currencies of different countries and enables comparison of international costs and prices. The major participants in this market are Commercial Banks, foreign exchange brokers and other authorised dealers and the monetary authorities.

20 **With reference to exchange rate, consider the following statements.** *(Chap 6, Class-XII, New NCERT)*

Statement-I Fixed exchange rate system is prone to speculative attacks on a currency.

Statement-II Government have to intervene to keep the exchange rate at the specified level even when there amount of reserve is inadequate and this may give rise to speculation of devaluation.

Which one of the following is correct in respect of the above statements?

(a) Both Statement-I and Statement-II are correct and Statement-II is the correct explanation for Statement-I.
(b) Both Statement-I and Statement-II are correct and Statement-II is not the correct explanation for Statement-I.
(c) Statement-I is correct, but Statement-II is incorrect.
(d) Statement-I is incorrect, but Statement-II is correct.

Ans. *(a)*

Exp. Both Statement-I and Statement-II are correct and Statement-II is the correct explanation for Statement-I. The fixed exchange rate system relies on government credibility to maintain specified rates. Deficits in the Balance of Payments (BoP) may necessitate intervention using official reserves. Inadequate reserves can trigger speculation, leading to devaluation.

Speculative attacks are common, as seen before the Bretton Woods System collapse.

In contrast, the flexible exchange rate system offers government flexibility without the need for substantial foreign exchange reserves.

Exchange rate movements automatically address BoP surpluses and deficits. Countries under this system gain independence in monetary policy as market forces regulate exchange rates, eliminating the need for constant government intervention.

21 **Which of the following statements is not correct about the Foreign Exchange Rate?**

(Chap 6, Class-XII, New NCERT)

(a) It can be determined through Flexible Exchange Rate, Fixed Exchange Rate or Managed Floating Exchange Rate.
(b) Flexible Exchange Rate is determined by the market forces of demand and supply.
(c) In the Dirty Floating Exchange Rate System, the government fixes the exchange rate at a particular level.
(d) Under the Managed Floating System, Central Banks intervene to buy and sell foreign currencies in an attempt to moderate exchange rate movements whenever they feel that such actions are appropriate.

Ans. (c)

Exp. Statement (c) is not correct about the Foreign Exchange Rate. The Managed Floating System of Exchange Rate is also called Dirty Floating Exchange Rate system.

22 **Consider the following statements regarding Fixed Exchange Rate System.** *(Chap 6, Class-XII, New NCERT)*

1. In a Fixed Exchange Rate System, when some government action increases, the exchange rate is called Revaluation.
2. Devaluation is said to occur when the government decreases the exchange rate in a Fixed Exchange Rate System.

Which of the statements given above is/are incorrect?

(a) Only 1
(b) Only 2
(c) Both 1 and 2
(d) Neither 1 nor 2

Ans. (c)

Exp. Both statements (1) and (2) are incorrect regarding Fixed Exchange Rate System.

Fixed Exchange Rate System is also known as Pegged Exchange Rate System and is characterised by devaluation and revaluation of the currency.

A devaluation is said to occur when the exchange rate is increased by government action under a Pegged Exchange Rate System. Devaluation makes domestic currency cheaper.

Where as revaluation is said to occur, when the government decreases the exchange rate, thereby making domestic currency costlier.

23 **Convertibility of rupee implies**

(Chap 6, Class-XII, New NCERT) (IAS Pre 2015)

(a) being able to convert rupee notes into gold.
(b) allowing the value of rupee to be fixed by market forces.
(c) freely permitting the conversion of rupee to other currencies and vice-versa.
(d) developing an international market for currencies in India.

Ans. (c)

Exp. Convertibility of rupee implies freely permitting the conversion of rupee to other currencies and vice-versa. India adopted full current account convertibility since 1993, permitting individuals and entities to convert Indian rupee into foreign currency.

24 **Which of the following is not one of the advantages of the Flexible Exchange Rate System?**

(Chap 6, Class-XII, New NCERT)

(a) The Flexible Exchange Rate System resolves problem of under valuation and overvaluation of currency.
(b) Government needs to maintain large stocks of foreign exchange reserves.
(c) Movements in the exchange rate automatically take care of the surpluses and deficits in the BoP.
(d) Countries gain independence in conducting their monetary policies, since they do not have to intervene to maintain exchange rates which are automatically taken care of by the market.

Ans. (b)

Exp. Statement (b) is not one of the advantages of the Flexible Exchange Rate System. In the Flexible Exchange Rate System, it is not necessary for the government to maintain a large stock of foreign exchange reserve.

Chapter 11

Liberalisation, Privatisation and Globalisation

Liberalisation, Privatisation and Globalisation

Liberalisation

Introduction

- Refers to a situation where unnecessary restrictions
- Indian economy was liberalised in the year 1991
- Expansion in role of private and foreign investment
- Restrictions were relaxed for private companies

Objectives

- To solve India's impending balance of payment crisis
- Increase the volume of foreign direct investment
- To maximise India's economic potential
- To usher in globalisation for Indian Economy

Measures

- De-regulation of Industrial Sector
- Financial Sector reforms
- Tax Reforms
- Foreign Exchange reforms
- Trade and Investment policy reforms

Privatisation

Introduction

- It implies shedding of the ownership
- Government made attempts to improve the efficiency of PSU
- Some PSUs have been granted special status

Objectives

- To reduce financial burden
- To improve public finances
- To encourage a wider share of ownership
- To de-politicise non-essential services

Disinvestment

- Privatisation implies a change in ownership, management
- Beyond 50% involves the transfer of management
- Minority Disinvestment
- Majority Disinvestment
- Below 50% would result to continuing undertaking

Globalisation

Introduction

- Understood to mean integration of the economy
- Outcome of the set up of various policies
- Involves creation of networks and activities

Effect

- Many Indian companies expanded their wings to other countries
- Increase in flow of investments from developed countries
- Technological development has resulted in reverse brain drain in India

Disadvantage

- The number of rural landless families increased from 35% to 45%
- Farmers are destined to die of starvation or suicide

Economic Reforms 1991 and Outcomes of LPG Reforms

Economic Reforms

- Changed the path of economy
- Referred as LPGM where M stands for Marketisation
- Introduced in 1991

Factors Responsible

- Rise in Prices – Rise in Fiscal Deficit
- Increase in Adverse Balance of Payments
- Iraq war
- Dismal performance of PSU
- Fall in foreign Exchange Reserves

Outcomes of LPG Reforms

Positive

- India's GDP growth rate increased
- After India adopted a New LPG policy, more employment generated
- Per capita income increased due to an increase in employment

Negative

- Share of agriculture in the GDP has gone down
- More MNL companies competed with local business
- LPG policies have led to widening income gaps
- Contributed the destruction of environment

SOURCE **New NCERT Class X** *(Globalisation and the Indian Economy),*
New NCERT Class XI *(Liberalisation, Privatisation and Globalisation : An Appraisal)*

1 With reference to the Indian economy in 1980s, consider the following statements.

(Chap 3, Class-XI, New NCERT)

1. Government halted spending on development programmes when revenue was very low.
2. Government was spending significant income on areas which were not providing immediate returns.
3. Government takes extensive measures to reduce profligate spending.

How many statements given above are correct?

(a) Only one (b) Only two
(c) All three (d) None of these

Ans. (a)

Exp. Only one statement i.e., (2) is correct with reference to the Indian economy in 1980s. The Indian Government, in 1980s, was spending a large share of its income on areas which don't provide immediate returns such as the social sector and defense.

Statements (1) and (3) are incorrect because government continued spending on development programmes when the revenue dipped low. Such spending did not generate additional revenue.

2 With reference to the Economic recession of 1991, consider the following statements.

(Chap 3, Class-XI, New NCERT)

1. In 1991, India met with an economic crisis relating to its internal debt.
2. The government was not able to make repayments on its borrowings from abroad.
3. Foreign exchange reserves maintained to import petroleum and other important items, dropped to levels that were not sufficient for even a fortnight.
4. The crisis was further compounded by rising prices of essential goods.

How many statements given above are incorrect?

(a) Only one (b) Only two
(c) All three (d) None of these

Ans. (a)

Exp. Only one statement i.e., (1) is incorrect with reference to the Economic recession of 1991. In 1991, India met with an economic crisis relating to its external debt (not internal debt) in which the government was not able to make repayments on its borrowings from abroad.

Foreign exchange reserves, maintained to import petroleum and other important items, dropped to levels that were not sufficient for even a fortnight.

The crisis was further compounded by rising prices of essential goods. All these led the government to introduce a new set of policy reforms in the country.

3 With reference to the Indian economy in 1990s, consider the following statements.

(Chap 3, Class-XI, New NCERT)

1. Loans provided to India from International Bank Reconstruction and Development (IBRD) were based on certain conditions.
2. India received $7 billion as loan from the International Financial Institutions to mitigate the crisis.

How many statements given above is/are correct?

(a) Only 1 (b) Only 2
(c) Both 1 and 2 (d) Neither 1 nor 2

Ans. (c)

Exp. Both statements (1) and (2) are correct with reference to the Indian economy in 1990s.

For availing the loan, these international agencies expected India to liberalise and open up the economy by removing restrictions on the private sector, reduce the role of the government in many areas and remove trade restrictions between India and other countries.

India approached the International Bank for Reconstruction and Development (IBRD), popularly known as World Bank and the International Monetary Fund (IMF) and received $7 billion as loan to manage the crisis.

4 With reference to New Economic Policy, consider the following statements.

(Chap 3, Class-XI, New NCERT)

1. The thrust of the NEP was towards creating a more competitive environment in the economy and removing the barriers to entry and growth of firms.
2. Stabilisation measures are long-term measures, intended to correct some of the weaknesses that have developed in the balance of payments and to bring inflation under control.
3. Structural reform policies aimed at removing the rigidities in various segments of the Indian economy.

How many statements given above are incorrect?

(a) Only one (b) Only two
(c) All three (d) None of these

Ans. (a)

Exp. Only one statement i.e., (2) is incorrect with reference to New Economic Policy.

The stabilisation measures introduced as a part of NEP are short-term measures. It intended to correct some of the weaknesses that have developed in the balance of payments and to bring inflation under control New Economic Policy was launched in 1991 with the aim to open the door for global exposure.

In the New Economic Policy, the government reduced the import duties, opened a reserved sector for private players, dwelled Indian currency to increase exports. It is also known as LPG model of growth.

5 With reference to liberalisation of Indian economy under New Economic Policy, consider the following statements. *(Chap 3, Class-XI, New NCERT)*

1. Industrial licensing was abolished for almost all product categories except alcohol, cigarettes, hazardous chemicals, etc.
2. The only industries, which are now reserved for the public sector are a part of atomic energy generation and some core activities in railway transport.
3. Many goods produced by small scale industries have now been dereserved.
4. In most industries, the market has not been allowed to determine the prices.

How many statements given above are incorrect?

(a) Only one (b) Only two
(c) Only three (d) All of these

***Ans.* (a)**

Exp. Only one statement i.e., (4) is incorrect with reference to the Indian economy under New Economic Policy.

In liberalisation, the market factors determine the prices of goods and services, on the basis of demand supply.

Liberalisation was introduced as a part of New Economic Policy in 1991 to put an end to restrictions imposed on private capital and open various sectors of the economy.

6 Consider the following statements about liberalisation of financial sector reforms. *(Chap 3, Class-XI, New NCERT)*

1. One of the major aims of Financial Sector reforms is to increase the role of RBI as regulator.
2. Foreign Institutional Investors (FII), such as merchant bankers, mutual funds and pension funds, are now allowed to invest in Indian financial markets.

Which of the statements given above is/are incorrect?

(a) Only 1
(b) Only 2
(c) Both 1 and 2
(d) Neither 1 nor 2

***Ans.* (a)**

Exp. Statement (1) is incorrect about the liberalisation of financial sector reforms.

The financial sector reforms under the liberalisation measure of 1991, envisaged to reduce the role of RBI from regulator to facilitator of Financial Sector. Financial Sector is also allowed to take decisions on many matters without consulting the RBI. FIIs were also allowed with some regulation in financial market.

7 With reference to the liberalisation policies in the Trade and Investment Policy, consider the following statements. *(Chap 3, Class-XI, New NCERT)*

1. Liberalisation of the trade and investment regime was initiated to decrease international competitiveness of industrial production.
2. Dismantling quantitative restrictions on imports and exports.
3. Increase in tariff rate.
4. Imposition of licensing procedures for imports.

How many statements given above is/are correct?

(a) Only one
(b) Only two
(c) Only three
(d) All of the above

***Ans.* (a)**

Exp. Only one statement i.e., (2) is correct with reference to liberalisation policies in the Trade and Investment Policy.

Dismantling of quantitative restrictions on imports and exports is one of the liberalisation policies in trade and investment policy.

Statements (1), (3) and (4) are incorrect.

Liberalisation of trade and investment regime was initiated to increase international competitiveness of industrial production and also foreign investments and technology into the economy.

It also aimed for reduction of tariff rates and removal of licensing procedures for imports.

8 Which of the following statements is incorrect regarding the liberalisation of Licensing Policy? *(Chap 3, Class-XI, New NCERT)*

(a) Import licensing was abolished except in case of hazardous and environmentally sensitive industries.
(b) Qualitative restrictions on imports of manufactured consumer goods and agricultural products were also fully removed from April, 2001.
(c) Export duties have been removed to increase the competitive position of Indian goods in the international markets.
(d) None of the above

***Ans.* (b)**

Exp. Statement (b) is incorrect regarding the liberalisation of Licensing Policy as quantitative (not qualitative) restrictions on imports of manufactured consumer goods and agricultural products were also fully removed from April, 2001.

Under the Trade Policy Reforms, quantitative restrictions on imports and exports were abolished, tariff rates were reduced, licensing procedures for imports were removed and exports duties were removed to increase the competitive position of Indian goods in the international markets.

9 **With reference to the Indian economy after 1991 economic liberalisation, consider the following statements.** *(Chap 3, Class-XI, New NCERT), (IAS Pre 2020)*

1. Worker productivity (₹ per worker at 2004-2005 prices) increased in urban areas while it decreased in rural areas.
2. The percentage share of rural areas in the workforce steadily increased.
3. In rural areas, the growth in the non-farm economy increased.
4. The growth rate in rural employment decreased.

Select the correct answer by using the codes given below.

(a) 1 and 2 (b) 3 and 4 (c) Only 3 (d) 1, 2 and 4

Ans. (b)

Exp. Statements (3) and (4) are correct regarding Indian economy after 1991 economic liberalisation because the overall economy had grown, specific sectors (including non-farm activities) have experienced growth.

The growth rate in rural employment decreased the liberalisation policies have faced criticism for uneven distribution of benefits, including potential negative impacts on employment.

The statements (1) and (2) are incorrect while liberalisation has indeed contributed to overall economic growth, it's essential to recognise that the impact on worker productivity can vary across different sectors and regions. The rural workforce's share does not increased significantly.

10 **Which of the following has/have occurred in India after its liberalisation of economic policies in 1991?** *(Chap 9, Class-XI, Tamil Nadu Board) (IAS Pre 2017)*

1. Share of agriculture in GDP increased enormously.
2. Share of India's exports in world trade increased.
3. FDI inflows increased.
4. India's foreign exchange reserves increased enormously.

Select the correct answer using the codes given below.

(a) 1 and 4 (b) 2, 3 and 4
(c) 2 and 3 (d) All of these

Ans. (b)

Exp. Statements (2), (3) and (4) are correct with reference to changes in the Indian economy post liberalisation of economic policies in 1991.

The opening up of the economy has led to a rapid increase in foreign direct investment. FDI increased by 150% and foreign exchange reserves by 20 times.

The foreign investment which includes foreign direct investment and foreign institutional investment, has increased from about US $00 million in 1990-1991 to US $150 billion in 2003-2004. India is seen as a successful exporter of IT Software Auto Parts Textiles and Engineering Goods in the reform period.

Statement (1) is incorrect. India's agriculture sector has shown a gradual decline in contribution of Indian economy only 15% to the GDP from 29% in 1991.

11 **Identify the correct statement regarding privatisation.** *(Chap 3, Class-XI, New NCERT)*

(a) Government companies are converted into private companies by withdrawal of the government from ownership and management of public sector companies or by outright sale of public sector companies.
(b) The purpose of the sale, according to the government, was mainly to improve financial discipline and facilitate modernisation.
(c) It was also envisaged that private capital and managerial capabilities could be effectively utilised to improve the performance of the PSUs.
(d) All of the above

Ans. (d)

Exp. All the given statements are correct regarding privatisation.

Privatisation was introduced as one of the measures in New Economic Policy (NEP) 1991 to increase efficiency and competitiveness of the Indian Public Sector.

It aimed for increasing the productivity and competitiveness of the Indian Public Sector.

For this purpose, Government companies are converted into private companies by withdrawals of the government from ownership and management of public sector. Also, the sale of goods improves the financial discipline and the private capital utilised to improve the performance of the PSUs.

12 **With reference to disinvestment, consider the following statements.** *(Chap 3, Class-XI, New NCERT)*

1. A minority disinvestment is the one in which the government retains a majority stake in the company.
2. A majority disinvestment is the one in which the government retains a minority stake in the company.

Select the correct answer by using the codes given below.

(a) Only 1 (b) Only 2
(c) Both 1 and 2 (d) Neither 1 nor 2

Ans. (d)

Exp. Neither statements (1) nor (2) are correct with reference to the disinvestment.

A minority disinvestment is one such that, at the end of it, the government retains a majority stake in the company, typically greater than 51%, thus ensuring management control.

A majority disinvestment is one in which the government, post disinvestment, retains a minority stake in the company i.e., it sells off a majority stake.

13 Consider the following Assertion (A) and Reason (R) and choose the correct code. *(Chap 3, Class-XI, New NCERT)*

Assertion (A) Although globalisation is generally understood as integration of the economy of the country with the world economy, but it is a complex phenomenon.

Reason (R) It is an outcome of the set of various policies that are aimed at transforming the world towards greater interdependence and integration.

Codes

(a) Both A and R are true and R is the correct explanation of A.
(b) Both A and R are true, but R is not the correct explanation of A.
(c) A is true, but R is false.
(d) A is false, but R is true.

Ans. (a)

Exp. Both Assertion (A) and Reason (R) are true and Reason (R) is the correct explanation of Assertion (A). Globalisation implies integration of the economy of the country with the world economy. Simply it means, markets of one country is open for another.

However, it is a complex phenomenon. Also, globalisation is an outcome of the set of various policies involving creation of networks and activities transcending economic, social and geographical boundaries. These policies are aimed at transforming the world towards greater interdependence and integration.

14 Consider the following statements with respect to outsourcing as an outcome of globalisation. *(Chap 3, Class-XI, New NCERT)*

1. Outsourcing involves hiring regular services from external sources which was previously provided from within the country.
2. The low wage rates and availability of skilled manpower in India have made it a destination for global outsourcing in the post-reform period.

Which of the statements given above is/are correct?

(a) Only 1
(b) Only 2
(c) Both 1 and 2
(d) Neither 1 nor 2

Ans. (c)

Exp. Both the given statements are correct regarding outsourcing as an outcome of globalisation.

In outsourcing, a company hires regular service from external sources, mostly from other countries, which was previously provided internally or from within the country. The growth of Information Technology (IT) has intensified the process of outsourcing.

After the LPG reforms of 1991, most Multinational Corporations (MNCs), and even small companies, are outsourcing their services to India where labour can be availed at a cheaper cost with reasonable degree of skill and accuracy and thus low wage rates and availability of skilled manpower in India have made India a destination for global outsourcing in post return period.

15 Which one of the following sectors of the Indian economy got the highest growth in the term of GDP contribution after the adoption of LPG model of economic development? *(Chap 3, Class-XI, New NCERT), (BPSC Pre 2016)*

(a) Agricultural Sector
(b) Fishing and Forestry Sector
(c) Mining and Quarrying Sector
(d) Services Sector

Ans. (d)

Exp. The 'Services Sector' of the Indian economy got the highest growth in the term of GDP contribution after the adoption of LPG model of economic development. Its contribution to Indian GDP has grown to around 57% and it is the largest recipient of Foreign Direct Investment (FDI) in India.

16 With reference to the effects of LPG on agriculture, consider the following statements. *(Chap 3, Class-XI, Old NCERT)*

1. Public investment in the agriculture sector especially in infrastructure, which includes irrigation, power, roads, market linkages and research and extension has increased.
2. Tightening of quantitative restrictions on the imports of agricultural products.
3. There has been a shift from production for the domestic market towards production for the export market focusing on cash crops in lieu of production of food grains.

How many statements given above is/are incorrect?

(a) Only one (b) Only two
(c) All three (d) None of these

Ans. (b)

Exp. Only two statements i.e., (1) and (2) are incorrect with reference to the effects of LPG on agriculture.

After the introduction of these reforms, public investment in the agricultural sector especially in infrastructure, which includes irrigation, power, roads, market linkages and research and extension has not increased but decreased.

Reforms have not been able to benefit agriculture, where the growth rate has been decelerating. Lifting of the quantitative restrictions on the imports of agricultural products was one of the policy changes introduced for the agricultural sector.

17 Consider the following statements regarding the LPG reforms in industrial sector. *(Chap 3, Class-XI, New NCERT)*

1. Industrial growth has recorded a slowdown because of decreasing demand for industrial products due to various reasons such as cheaper imports, inadequate investment in infrastructure etc.
2. Globalisation is often seen as creating conditions for the free movement of goods and services from foreign countries that adversely affect the local industries and employment opportunities in developing countries.

Which of the statements given above is/are correct?

(a) Only 1 (b) Only 2
(c) Both 1 and 2 (d) Neither 1 nor 2

Ans. (c)

Exp. Both the given statements (1) and (2) are correct regarding the LPG reforms in industrial sector.

Globalisation is often seen as creating conditions for the free movement of goods and services from foreign countries that adversely affect the local industries and employment opportunities in developing countries.

Due to this, domestic manufacturers of India are facing competition from imports.

The slowdown of industrial growth is one of the negative impacts of LPG reforms. It was caused due to decreased demand for industrial products due to various reasons such as cheaper imports, inadequate investment in infrastructure, etc.

18 Which of the following statements is incorrect regarding the criticism of LPG Policy in the Indian economy? *(Chap 3, Class-XI, New NCERT)*

(a) The process of globalisation through liberalisation and privatisation policies has produced positive as well as negative results both for India and other countries.
(b) Globalisation should be seen as an opportunity in terms of greater access to global markets, high technology and increased possibility of large industries of developing countries to become important players in the international arena.
(c) Globalisation is a strategy of developed countries to expand their markets in other countries.
(d) The market-driven globalisation has widened the economic disparities among nations and people.

Ans. (b)

Exp. Statement (b) is incorrect regarding the criticism of LPG policy in the Indian economy.

Globalisation should be seen as an opportunity in terms of greater access to global markets, high technology and increased possibility for large industries of developing countries, to become important players in the international arena is one of the positive aspects of globalisation. It has integrated the economy of the country with the world economy.

19 With reference to LPG Reforms and Fiscal Policy, consider the following statements. *(Chap 3, Class-XI, New NCERT)*

1. Economic reforms have placed limits on the growth of public expenditure, especially in social sectors.
2. The tax reductions in the reform period, aimed at yielding larger revenue and curb tax evasion, have not resulted in an increase in tax revenue for the government.
3. The reform policies involving tariff reduction have increased the scope for raising revenue through custom duties.

How many statements given above is/are incorrect?

(a) Only one (b) Only two
(c) Only three (d) None of these

Ans. (a)

Exp. Only one statement i.e., (3) is incorrect with reference to LPG Reforms and Fiscal Policy. One of the negative fallouts of LPG reforms in context of fiscal policies is that, the reform policies involving tariff reduction, have curtailed the scope for raising revenue through custom duties. It has created a negative impact on developmental and welfare expenditures.

20 Which of the following sector is/are now reserved for the public sector in India? *(Chap 3, Class-XII, NCERT)*

1. Atomic energy generation
2. Some core activities in railway
3. Petroleum products

Codes

(a) 1 and 2 (b) 2 and 3 (c) 1 and 3 (d) 1, 2 and 3

Ans. (a)

Exp. Atomic energy generation and some core activities in railway are reserved for the public sector in India. Due to New Economic Policy (NEP) 1991, as of now just two sectors of national importance are reserved for the public enterprises.

21 Which among the following given factor(s) has/ have enabled the process of globalisation? *(Chap 4, Class-X, New NCERT)*

1. Increased use of technology
2. Liberalisation of foreign trade and foreign investment policy
3. Removing barriers or restrictions set by the government

Codes

(a) Only 1 (b) 1 and 2 (c) 1, 2 and 3 (d) 1 and 3

Ans. (c)

Exp. All the given factors have enabled the process of globalisation. Increased use of technology, liberalisation of foreign trade and foreign investment policy and removing barriers or restrictions set by the government are considered as some of the factors that have enabled globalisation.

Chapter 12

International Organisations

International Organisations

World Bank Group
- Family of five international organisation
- Provide loans to developing countries
- Largest bank of the world

International Bank for Reconstruction and Development (IBRD)
- Provides loans to middle income credit worthy poor countries
- Created in 1944 to help Europe

International Development Association (IDA)
- Aims to reduce poverty
- One of the largest sources to assistance
- Lends money on concessional term

International Finance Corporation
- To achieve more economic development
- Invest in private enterprises
- To stimulate conditions conductive to the flow of private capital

Multilateral Investment Guarantee Agency (MIGA)
- Offers political risk insurance
- Established in 1988
- Target projects that endevour to create new job

International Monetary Fund (IMF)
- Concieved at UN conference
- Works to foster global monetary cooperation
- It become special agency of UN in

World Trade Organisation (WTO)
- Successor to the General Agreement on (GATT)
- Created on 1st January, 1995
- Headquarters in Geneva Switzerland
- Dealing with the rules of trade between nations

United Nations Conference on trade and Development (UNCTAD)
- Established in 1964
- Promoting the development friendly integration
- To maximise the trade and investment

World Economic Forum (WEF)
- A swiss non profit foundation
- Established in 1971
- Recognised by the swiss authorities
- To improve the state of the world

G-7
- Organisation of 7 non socialist countries
- Adopting free market policies in economy
- Members are USA, Canada, Germany, Britain, France, Italy and Japan

G-20
- An informal group of 19 countries and European Union
- Its origin can be tracked back to 1997-1999
- Spain also attends leader summit as a permanent non-member
- Established in 1919

Asia-Pacific Economic Cooperation (APEC)
- A regional economic forum
- Promote sustainable growth and economic relation
- India is not a member of APEC

Brazil-Russia-India-China-South Africa (BRICS)
- First summit was held in Yekaterinburg
- Term was coined by economist JIM 'O' Neil

South Asian Association for Regional Co-operation (SAARC)
- Founded in 1985; Promote the welfare of the people of South Asia; Established to contribute to mutual trust

Association of South-East Asian Nations (ASEAN)
- Established in 1967 in Bangkok
- Promote active collabration on matters of common interest in the economic

Asian Infrastructure Investment Bank (AIIB)
- Mission to improve social and economics outcomes in ASIA
- Headquarters in Beijing
- Begin its operation in January 2016

Asian Development Bank (ADB)
- Established on 19th December 1966
- ADB has 68 members, 49 from Asia
- Promote social and economic development in Asia

New Development Bank (NDB)
- Founded by BRICS countries
- Formed to support infrastructure efforts in BRICS; Headquarters at Sanghai, also known as BRICS Bank

SOURCE **Old NCERT Class IX & X** *(Towards Economic Development)*, **New NCERT Class X** *(Globalisation and the Indian Economy)*, **New NCERT Class X** *(Development)*, **New NCERT Class XI** *(Liberalisation, Privatisation and Globalisation : An Appraisal)*, **New NCERT Class XI** *(Comparative Development Experiences of Indian and Its Neighbours)*, **New NCERT Class XII** *(Our Economy : Macroeconomics)*

1 **Consider the following statements regarding the World Trade Organisation.** *(Chap 4, Class-X, New NCERT)*

1. The WTO was founded in 1948 as the Predecessor Organisation to the GATT.
2. GATT was established in 1995 with 3 countries as the Global Trade organisation to administer all multilateral trade agreements by providing equal opportunities to all countries in the international market for trading purposes.
3. WTO aims to establish a rule-based trading regime in which nations cannot place arbitrary restriction on trade.
4. WTO has 164 members and 24 observer governments.

How many of the statements given above is/are incorrect?

(a) Only one (b) Only two
(c) All three (d) None of these

Ans. (b)

Exp. Only two statements i.e., (1) and (2) are incorrect as the WTO was founded in 1995 as the successor organisation to the GATT (General Agreement on Trade and Tariff). GATT was established in 1948 with 23 countries as the Global Trade organisation to administer all multilateral trade agreements by providing equal opportunities to all countries in the international market for trading purpose.

2 **Consider the following statements about the World Trade Organisation (WTO).** *(Chap 3, Class-XI, New NCERT)*

1. As an important member of WTO, India has been in the forefront of framing fair global rules, regulations and safeguards and advocating the interests of the developing world.
2. India has kept its commitments towards liberalisation of trade, made in the WTO, by removing quantitative restrictions on imports and reducing tariff rates.
3. Its purpose is to remove tariff as well as non-tariff barriers and provide greater market access to all member countries.

How many of the statements given above are correct?

(a) Only one (b) Only two
(c) All three (d) None of these

Ans. (c)

Exp. All the three given statements i.e., (1), (2) and (3) are correct about the WTO. India has been a WTO member since 1st January, 1995. As an important member of WTO, India has been in the forefront of framing fair rules, regulations and safeguards and advocating the interest of developing world.

India has kept its commitments towards liberalisation of trade, made in the WTO, by removing quantitative restrictions on imports and reducing tariff rates.

For instance, one of the specific features of Export-Import Policy (2000-2001) of India was the removal of quantitative restrictions within the provisions of WTO. The main purpose of WTO is to remove trade barriers and provide greater market access to all member countries.

3 **Consider the following statements about the World Trade Organisation (WTO).** *(Chap 3, Class-XI, New NCERT)*

1. Its purpose is also to enlarge production and trade of services, to ensure optimum utilisation of world resources and to protect the environment.
2. The WTO agreements unlike GATT cover trade in goods only.

Which of the statements given above is/are incorrect?

(a) Only 1 (b) Only 2
(c) Both 1 and 2 (d) Neither 1 nor 2

Ans. (b)

Exp. Statement (2) is incorrect because the WTO agreements cover trade in goods and services to facilitate international trade (bilateral and multilateral) through removal of tariff as well as non-tariff barriers and providing greater market access to all member countries.

4 **Which of the following statements is incorrect regarding the International Monetary Fund (IMF)?** *(Chap 4, Class-IX & X, Old NCERT)*

1. It is a specialised agency of the United Nations.
2. It has reserves of currencies of all countries, which are deposited by the respective countries according to their fixed quota.
3. It cannot fulfill the unexpected demand for foreign currencies.
4. It assists in providing stability in the foreign exchange rates.

Codes

(a) 1 and 4 (b) Only 2 (c) Only 3 (d) 1, 2 and 3

Ans. (c)

Exp. Statement (3) is incorrect regarding the IMF because it assists countries in providing stability in the foreign exchange rates by providing foreign currencies when unexpected demand arises. It also assists countries in case of Balance of Payment Crisis and works towards achieving macroeconomic stability in the world.

International Monetary Fund (IMF) was formed in 1944 at the Bretton Woods Conference.

5 **Consider the following statements.** *(Chap 7, Class-XI, Tamil Nadu Board)*

1. The formation of the IMF (International Monetary Fund) was initiated in 1944 at the Bretton Woods Conference.
2. IMF focuses on fostering global monetary co-operation, securing financial stability and facilitating and promoting international trade,

employment and economic growth around the world.

3. India holds 2.75 percent of SDR quota, and 2.63 percent of votes in the IMF.

How many of the above statements is/are correct?

(a) Only one
(b) Only two
(c) All three
(d) None of these

Ans. (c)

Exp. All three statements i.e., (1), (2) and (3) are correct. The International Monetary Fund (IMF) is a large international organisation with 190 members countries. It established in 1944 at the Bretton Woods Conference with the primary goal of promoting global financial stability and facilitating international trade. As of October 2021, India holds 2.75% of the total Special Drawing Rights (SDRS) and 2.63% percent of votes in the IMF.

6 Regarding the IMF which one of the following statements is correct? *(Chap 4, Class-X, New NCERT)* *(IAS Pre 2011)*

(a) It can grant loans to any country
(b) It can grants loans to only developed countries
(c) It grants loans to only member countries
(d) It can grant loans to the central bank of a country

Ans. (c)

Exp. Statement (c) is correct regarding IMF.

International Monetary Fund grants loans to its member countries (not to any country).

It also grants loans to developing countries not only developed country. It does not grant loans to central bank of a country.

7 Consider the following statements with respect to International Monetary Fund (IMF). *(Chap 6, Class-XII, New NCERT)*

1. Its calculation of the Special Drawing Rights is based on Euro, Japanese Yen, Dollar, Pound Sterling and Dinar.
2. The original installments of SDRs were distributed to member countries according to their quota in the fund.

Which of the statements given above is/are incorrect?

(a) Only 1
(b) Only 2
(c) Both 1 and 2
(d) Neither 1 nor 2

Ans. (a)

Exp. Statement (1) is incorrect with respect to IMF because calculation of the Special Drawing Rights (SDR) of IMF is based on weighted sum of five currencies, namely US Dollar, the Euro, the Chinese Renminbi, the Japanese Yen and the British Pound Sterling. It is an international reserve asset created by IMF to supplement the official reserves of its member countries.

8 Analyse the following statements about the reserve tranche. *(Chap 4, Class-X, Old NCERT)*

1. The reserve tranche is a portion of a country's quota contribution to the IMF that it can access without conditions.
2. It serves as a safety net for countries facing temporary balance of payments difficulties.
3. Countries are only eligible for the reserve tranche if they have a good credit rating.

How many of the statements given above is/are incorrect?

(a) Only one
(b) Only two
(c) All three
(d) None of these

Ans. (a)

Exp. Only one statements i.e., (3) is incorrect as the reserve tranches that countries hold with the IMF are considered their facilities of first resort, meaning they will tap into the reserve tranche before seeking a formal credit tranche.

9 Consider the following statements. *(Chap 8, Class-XI, Tamil Nadu Board)*

1. BRICS is the acronym for an association of 5-major emerging national economies. Brazil, Russia, India, China and South Africa.
2. BRICS members encompass about 30% of the World's land surface and 45% of the global population.

Which of the statements given above is/are incorrect?

(a) Only 1
(b) Only 2
(c) Both 1 and 2
(d) Neither 1 nor 2

Ans. (d)

Exp. Neither statements (1) nor (2) are incorrect as BRICS is acronym for an association of 5-major emerging national economies Brazil, Russia, India, China and South Africa.

The founding countries of Brazil, Russia, India and China held the first summit in Yekaterinburg in 2009, with South Africa joining the bloc a year later. Egypt, Ethiopia, Iran and the United Arab Emirates joined the organisation on 1st January 2024. Combined, the BRICS members encompass about 30% of the world's land surface and 45% of the global population.

10 Consider the following statements. *(Chap 4, Class-X, New NCERT)*

1. International Labour Organisation (ILO) was established in 1919 by the Treaty of Versailles.
2. It promotes internationally recognised human and labour rights.
3. There are eight core conventions of the ILO.

How many of the above statements is/are correct?

(a) Only one
(b) Only two
(c) All three
(d) None of these

Ans. (c)

Exp. All three statements i.e., (1), (2) and (3) are correct. The International Labour Organisation (ILO) is a United Nations agency, promotes internationally recognised human and labour rights. It was founded in October 1919 and has 187 member states. It is headquartered in Geneva, Switzerland. There are eight conventions of ILO. For example, forced labour convention, minimum age convention, etc.

11 India is a member of which of the following organisations? *(Glossary, Class-XI ,New NCERT)*

1. Association of South-East Asian Nations (ASEAN).
2. The South Asian Association for Regional Cooperation (SAARC).
3. G-7

Codes

(a) 1 and 3 (b) 1 and 2 (c) Only 2 (d) 1, 2 and 3

Ans. (c)

Exp. Statement (2) is correct. India is the member of the South Asian Association for Regional Cooperation (SAARC). It is an association of eight countries of South Asia, namely, Bangladesh, Bhutan, India, Maldives, Nepal, Pakistan, Sri Lanka and Afghanistan. It provides a platform for the peoples of South Asia to work together in a spirit of friendship, trust and understanding.

While India is not the member of ASEAN and G-7.

12 Which of the following countries is not a member of the European Union? *(Glossary, Class-X, New NCERT)*

1. France 2. Lithuania 3. Germany 4. Russia

Codes

(a) Only 1 and 2 (b) Only 2 and 3
(c) Only 3 and 4 (d) Only 4

Ans. (d)

Exp. Russia is not a member of the European Union. European Union is a union of 27 member states that are located primarily in Europe. It was founded to enhance political, economic and social cooperation within the European continent.

13 Which of the following is not associated with NAFTA? *(Chap 9, Class-XII, New NCERT) (BPSC Pre 2018)*

1. Great Britain 2. Canada
3. Mexico 4. USA

How many of the above statements are correct?

(a) Only 1 (b) Only 2
(c) Only 1, 2 and 3 (d) Only 1, 2 and 4

Ans. (a)

Exp. Great Britain is not associated with the North American Free Trade Association (NAFTA). It is a multilateral trading organisation founded by United States, Canada and Mexico in 1994.

It is one of the largest trade blocs in the world in terms of gross domestic product. On 1st July, 2020, NAFTA was replaced by US-Mexico-Canada Agreement (USMCA).

14 Consider the following statements with respect to SAARC. *(Glossary, Class-XI, New NCERT)*

1. It comprises of seven South Asian countries.
2. The main objectives of SAARC is social and economic development of the member countries.

Which of the statements given above is/are incorrect?

(a) Only 1 (b) Only 2
(c) Both 1 and 2 (d) Neither 1 nor 2

Ans. (b)

Exp. Statement (1) is incorrect. SAARC is an association of eight countries of South Asia—Bangladesh, Bhutan, India, Maldives, Nepal, Pakistan, Sri Lanka and Afghanistan.

15 Which of the following statements is incorrect about G-20? *(Glossary, Class-XI, New NCERT)*

1. It works to promote international financial stability and sustainable development.
2. India is a member nation of G-20.
3. The European Union is not a member of this organisation.

Codes

(a) Only one (b) Only two
(c) Al three (d) None of these

Ans. (a)

Exp. Only one statement i.e., (3) is incorrect about G-20 because the European Union is the member of G-20. It is represented by the President of the European Council and head of European Central Bank.

G-20 is a forum of countries that intents to promote global economic stability and sustainable growth.

India is also the member of G-20. The other members of G-20 besides India and European Union are Argentina, Australia, Brazil, Japan, South Korea, Mexico, Russia, Saudi Arabia, South Africa, Turkey, United Kingdom, USA, Canada, China, France, Germany, Indonesia, Italy.

16 Why was the World Bank established? *(Chap 7, Class-XI, Tamil Nadu Board)*

(a) To promote the International Trade
(b) To reconstruct the economies damaged during the Second World War
(c) To improve the adverse Balance of Payment situation of the non-member countries
(d) None of the above

Ans. (b)

Exp. The prime motive behind the establishment of the World Bank was to provide long-run capital to member countries for economic reconstruction and development of the economies ruined by the Second World War.

The World Bank was established in 1944 at the Bretton Woods Conference. Its original mission was to provide loans to countries that had been devastated by the second World War.

The World Bank also provided technical assistance to help these countries rebuild their economies.

Practice Set (1-3)

- Practice Set-1
- Practice Set-2
- Practice Set-3

Practice Set 01

1 **Consider the following statements.** *(IAS Pre 2021)*

1. The Governor of the Reserve Bank of India (RBI) is appointed by the Central Government.
2. Certain provisions in the Constitution of India provide the Central Government the right to issue directions to the RBI in public interest.
3. The Governor of the RBI draws his power from the RBI Act.

Which of the above statements is/are correct?

(a) 1 and 2 (b) 2 and 3
(c) 1 and 3 (d) 1, 2 and 3

2 **In the context of finance, the term 'Beta' refers to** *IAS (Pre) 2023*

(a) the process of simultaneous buying and selling of an asset from different platforms
(b) an investment strategy of portfolio manager to balance risk versus reward
(c) a type of systemic risk that arises where perfect hedging is not possible
(d) a numeric value that measures the fluctuations of a stock to changes in the overall stock market

In India, the Central Bank function as the 'lender of last resort' usually refers to which of the following? *(IAS Pre 2021)*

1. Lending to trade and industry bodies when they fail to borrow from other sources.
2. Providing liquidity to the banks having a temporary crisis.
3. Lending to governments to finance budgetary deficits.

Select the correct answer using the codes given below

(a) 1 and 2 (b) Only 2 (c) 2 and 3 (d) Only 3

With reference to 'Urban Cooperative Banks' in India, consider the following statements. *(IAS Pre 2021)*

1. They are supervised and regulated by local boards set-up by the State Governments.
2. They can issue equity shares and preference shares.
3. They were brought under the purview of the Banking Regulation Act, 1949 through an Amendment in 1966.

Which of the statements given above is/are correct?

(a) Only 1 (b) 2 and 3
(c) 1 and 3 (d) 1, 2 and 3

5 **With reference to India, consider the following statements.** *(IAS Pre 2021)*

1. Retail investors through demat account can invest in 'Treasury Bills' and 'Government of India Debt Bonds' in primary market.
2. The 'Negotiated Dealing System-Order Matching' is a government securities trading platform of the Reserve Bank of India.
3. The 'Central Depository Services Ltd.' is jointly promoted by the Reserve Bank of India and the Bombay Stock Exchange.

Which of the statements given above is/are correct?

(a) Only 1 (b) 1 and 2 (c) Only 3 (d) 2 and 3

6 **Which of the following measures would result in an increase in the money supply in the economy?** *(IAS Pre 2012)*

1. Purchase of government securities from the public by the Central Bank.
2. Deposit of currency in commercial banks by the public.
3. Borrowing by the government from the Central Bank.
4. Sale of government securities to the public by the Central Bank.

Codes

(a) Only 1 (b) 2 and 4 (c) 1 and 3 (d) 2, 3 and 4

7 **Consider the following statements.**

1. Atal Pension Yojana is operated by department of finance services.
2. There is no minimum or maximum income limit to join Atal Pension Scheme.
3. Unorganised sector workers with monthly income upto fifteen thousand can only join Pradhan Mantri Shram Yogi Maandhan yojana.
4. Ministry of Labour and Employment operates Pradhan Mantri Shram Yogi Maandhan Yojana.

How many of the statements given above is/are correct?

(a) Only one (b) Only two
(c) Only three (d) None of these

8 **Consider the following statements.**

1. Progressive taxation takes large percentage of tax from high income individuals.
2. Capital gain tax is a direct tax.
3. Surcharge is considered as tax on tax.

**These practice sets also include important NCERT based previous years' questions of IAS and State PSC examination.*

Which of the statements given above is/are correct?
(a) Only 3 (b) 1 and 3
(c) All of these (d) None of these

9 **Consider the following statements.**
Statement-I Interest for Marginal Standing facility is Repo rate plus 1%.
Statement-II Prompt corrective action are quantitative tools of RBI.
Which one of the following is correct in respect of the above statements?
(a) Both Statement-I and Statement-II are correct and Statement-II is the correct explanation for Statement-I.
(b) Both Statement-I and Statement-II are correct and Statement-II is not the correct explanation for Statement-I.
(c) Statement-I is correct but Statement-II is incorrect.
(d) Statement-I is incorrect but Statement-II is correct.

10 **Consider the following statements regarding Indian Planning.** *(IAS Pre 2009)*
1. The Second Five-Year Plan emphasised on the establishment of heavy industries.
2. The Third Five-Year Plan introduced the concept of import substitution as a strategy for industrialisation.

Which of the statements given above is/are correct?
(a) Only 1 (b) Only 2
(c) Both 1 and 2 (d) Neither 1 nor 2

11 **Consider the following statements.**
1. Mining is a primary sector activity.
2. Uber is an example of Gig economy.
3. Poultry farming is a secondary sector activity.
4. A doctor in India advising patient of Dubai, is an example of service exports.

Which of the statements given above is/are correct?
(a) 1 and 2 (b) 2 and 3 (c) 1, 2 and 4 (d) 1, 2 and 3

12 **Consider the following pairs.**
1. Demand Liabilities – Fixed deposits
2. Time Liabilities – Current deposits
3. Imperial Bank of India – SBI
4. Urjit Patel Committee – MSME

How many of the above pairs is/are correctly matched?
(a) Only one (b) Only two (c) Only three (d) All four

13 **Which of following statements about non-plan expenditures of the Central Government is correct?** *69th BPSC (Pre) 2023*
(a) The expenditure is on interest payments.
(b) The expenditure is on science and technology
(c) The expenditure is on agriculture.
(d) None of the above

14 **Which is not the purpose of forming Banks Board Bureau?**
1. The bureau will recommend appointment of senior officials in public-sector banks from government interference.
2. The bureau will inspect the level of NPAs of public-sector banks.
3. The bureau will identify the best practices in private-sector banks and seek their implementation in public sector banks.

Codes
(a) Only 1 (b) 2 and 3
(c) 1 and 2 (d) 1, 2 and 3

15 **Consider the following statements.** *IAS (Pre) 2023*
Statement 1 India accounts for 3.2% of global export of goods.
Statement 2 Many local companies and foreign companies operating in India have taken advantage of India's Production Linked Incentive (PLI) Scheme.

Codes
(a) Both statements 1 and 2 are correct and statement 2 is the correct explanation for statement 1.
(b) Both statements 1 and 2 are correct and statements 2 is not the correct explanation for statement 1.
(c) Statement 1 is correct but statement 2 is incorrect.
(d) Statement 1 is incorrect but statement 2 is correct.

16 **With reference to the Indian Economy, consider the following statements.** *(IAS Pre 2022)*
1. If the inflation is too high, Reserve Bank of India (RBI) is likely to buy government securities.
2. If the rupee is rapidly depreciating, RBI is likely to sell dollars in the market.
3. If interest rates in the USA or European Union were to fall, that is likely to induce RBI to buy dollars.

Which of the statements given above is/are correct?
(a) 1 and 2
(b) 2 and 3
(c) 1 and 3
(d) 1, 2 and 3

17 **The Foreign Exchange Reserves (FER) of RBI include which of the following?**
1. Foreign Currency Assets (FCA)
2. Gold
3. Special Drawing Right (SDR)
4. Reserve Tranche Position (RTP)

Select the correct answer using the codes given below.
(a) 1 and 2 (b) 2, 3 and 4
(c) 1, 2 and 3 (d) All of these

18 **Consider the following statements.**
1. More than 55% of the people in India are directly or indirectly dependent on agriculture.
2. Industrial sector contributes 33% in India's GDP.
3. Dairy and Poultry sector contributes 11% to GDP of India.

How many of the statements given above is/are correctly matched?
(a) Only one (b) Only two
(c) All three (d) None of these

19 **Consider the following statements and identify correct ones.**
1. Reduction in repo rate increase money multiplier.
2. Reduction in Case Reserve Ratio By RBI indicates less risk awaited assets with banks.

Codes
(a) Only 1 (b) Only 2
(c) Both 1 and 2 (d) None of these

20 **Consider the following pairs.**

	Institutions	Year (Establishment)
1.	IBRD	1944
2.	IFD	1948
3.	IDA	1960
4.	MIGA	1988

How many of the above pairs is/are correctly matched?
(a) Only one (b) Only two
(c) Only three (d) All of these

21 **Devaluation of a currency means**
(a) reduction in the value of a currency vis-a-vis major internationally traded currencies.
(b) permitting the currency to seek its worth in the international market.
(c) fixing the value of the currency in conjunction with the movement in the value of a basket of predetermined currencies.
(d) fixing the value of a currency in multilateral consultation with the IMF, the World Bank and major trading partners.

22 **Which of the following statements is/are correct?**
1. Whole Sale Price Index measure the change in the price of goods sold and traded in bulk.
2. Consumer Price Index is calculated by Office of Economic Advisor.

Codes
(a) Only 1
(b) Only 2
(c) Both 1 and 2
(d) None of the above

23 **Consider the following statement with reference to "Nandini Krishak Samriddhi Yojana"**
1. This scheme includes milch cow breeds of Sahiwal, Gir, Tharparkar and Gangatiri only.
2. Beneficiary must have at least one year of cattle rearing experience.

Codes
(a) Neither 1 nor 2 (b) Only 2
(c) Only 1 (d) Both 1 and 2

24 **Consider the following pairs.**
1. WTO – Multilateral trade negotiation body
2. IDA – Provides loans to address short-term balance of payment problems
3. IMF – Sanction of soft loans
4. IBRD – Facilitating lending and borrows for reconstruction and development

How many of the above pairs is/are correctly matched?
(a) Only one (b) Only two (c) Only three (d) All four

25 **Which of the following statement is incorrect?**
(a) Balance of Payment is a systematic statement of all economic transactions of a country with the rest of the world.
(b) Gold reserves with RBI are not part of Forex reserves.
(c) Increase in inflation rate can increase the demand for foreign currency.
(d) Rate at which one country's currency exchanges for a basket of multiple foreign currencies is Nominal Exchange Rate.

26 **Consider the following statements regarding post-liberalisation India's balance of payments position.**
1. The current account deficit is on account of net import of services.
2. The capital account surplus is on account of large amount of external assistance received on bilateral basis.
3. The balance of payments situation has improved post-liberalisation.

How many of the statements given above is/are correct?
(a) Only one (b) Only two
(c) All three (d) None of these

27 **With refrerence of the Ministry, consider the following pairs.**
1. Darpan Portal – NITI Aayog
2. POSHAN Abhiyan – Ministry of Women and Development
3. Base Year for Consumer Price Index – 2015
4. SAUBHAGYA Scheme – Ministry of Power

How many of the above pairs is/are correctly matched?
(a) Only one (b) Only two (c) Only three (d) All four

28 **Consider the following statements.**
1. Samarth Udyog Bharat 4.0 aims to promote technological solutions to Indian manufacturing units to make them ready for industry 4.0 by 2025.
2. Recovery and recycling is a part of circular economic model.
3. National policy on electronics targets $400 from electronic manufacturing by 2025.

Which of the statements given above is/are correct?
(a) Only 1
(b) 2 and 3
(c) All of these
(d) None of the above

29 **Which of the following statements is/are correct regarding FDI under automatic route?**
1. FDI in India under the automatic route does not require prior approval either by the Government of India or the Reserve Bank of India.
2. Investors are only required to notify the concerned regional office of the RBI before receipt of inward remittances and file required documents with the office before the issue of shares to foreign investors.

Codes
(a) Only 1 (b) Only 2
(c) Both 1 and 2 (d) Neither 1 nor 2

30 **Which of the following statement is not true?**
(a) The World Trade Organisation (WTO) requires member nations to give national treatment to international goods and services.
(b) The General Agreement on Tariffs and Trade (GATT) was replaced by the World Trade Organisation (WTO) in 1995.
(c) The most favoured nation principle under GATT provided that preferential trading agreements reached with one country should be extended to other countries.
(d) The WTO has been able to cover in its agreements the direct taxation policies of member nations.

Practice Set 02

1 **With reference to Indian economy, demand pull-inflation can be caused/increased by which of the following?** *(IAS Pre 2021)*
1. Expansionary policies
2. Fiscal stimulus
3. Inflation-indexing wages
4. Higher-purchasing power
5. Rising interest rates

Select the correct answer using the codes given below.
(a) 1, 2 and 4 (b) 3, 4 and 5
(c) 1, 2, 3 and 5 (d) 1, 2, 3, 4 and 5

2 **With reference to the casual workers employed in India, consider the following statements.** *(IAS Pre 2021)*
1. All casual workers are entitled for Employees Provident Fund coverage.
2. All casual workers are entitled for regular working hours and overtime payment.
3. The government can by a notification specify that an establishment or industry shall pay wages only through its bank account.

Which of the above statements is/are correct?
(a) 1 and 2 (b) 2 and 3
(c) 1 and 3 (d) 1, 2 and 3

3 **Consider the following pairs.** *Telangana PCS (Pre) 2023*

Iron and Steel Plant		State
1. Bhilai	–	Chhattisgarh
2. Bokaro	–	Jharkhand
3. Dolvi	–	Maharashtra
4. Daitari	–	Odisha

Codes
(a) 1 and 2 (b) 2 and 3
(c) 1, 2 and 4 (d) All of these

4 **Consider the following statements.**
Statement-I Many industries in India have obtained ISO 9001 and ISO 9002 Certification in the recent past.
Statement-II There has been considerable liberalisation in the licensing policy of the Government of India.

Which one of the following is correct in respect of the above statements?
(a) Both Statement-I and Statement-II are correct and Statement-II is the correct explanation for Statement-I.
(b) Both Statement-I and Statement-II are correct and Statement-II is not the correct explanation for Statement-I.
(c) Statement-I is correct but Statement-II is incorrect.
(d) Statement-I is incorrect but Statement-II is correct.

5 **Other things remaining unchanged, market demand for a good might increase if** *(IAS Pre 2021)*

1. Price of its substitute increases.
2. Price of its complement increases.
3. The good is an inferior good and income of the consumers increases.
4. Its price falls.

Which of the above statements is/are correct?

(a) 1 and 4 (b) 2, 3 and 4
(c) 1, 3 and 4 (d) 1, 2 and 3

6 **Consider the following.**

1. Currency with the public
2. Demand deposits with banks
3. Time deposits with banks

How many of the above is/are included in Broad Money (M3)?

(a) Only one (b) Only two
(c) All three (d) None of these

7 **Consider the following statements.**

1. Near money is an asset that is highly liquid and can be readily converted into cash.
2. A promissory note is legal financial tool declared by a party promising another to pay the debt on a particular day.

Which of the statements given above is/are correct?

(a) Only 1 (b) Only 2
(c) Both 1 and 2 (d) Neither 1 nor 2

8 **Which of the following statement regarding iron-ore in Madhya Pradesh is not correct?** *MPPSC (Pre) 2023*

(a) Madhya Pradesh ranks third in the country in the production of iron-ore.
(b) The hematite deposits are in the North-Eastern of Jabalpur district.
(c) Content of mica and silica is high in these deposits.
(d) The iron-ore reserve have been reduced after the separation of Chhattisgarh State.

9 **Which of the following statements is/are correct?**

1. Indian Renewable Energy Development Agency (IREDA) launched India's first Masala bond at London Stock Exchange.
2. Seychelles issued world's first 'Blue Bond'.
3. Paid up capital is amount paid by shareholders for the share held by them in company.

How many of the above statements is/are correct?

(a) Only one (b) Only two
(c) All three (d) None of these

10 **Which of the following statements is/are incorrect?**

1. Venture capital is a type of private equity use to finance emerging firms that have growth potential.
2. Insurance companies are liability driven financial intermediaries.

Codes

(a) Only 1 (b) Only 2
(c) Both 1 and 2 (d) Neither 1 nor 2

11 **Consider the following statements.**

1. NIRVIK is an Export Credit Insurance Scheme operated by Ministry of Commerce through Export Credit Guarantee Corporation (ECGC).
2. Motor Vehicle Act, 1988 requires all motor vehicle owners to purchase third party insurance.

Which of the statements given above is/are correct?

(a) Only 1
(b) Only 2
(c) Both 1 and 2
(d) Neither 1 nor 2

12 **Consider the following statements.**

1. Post office saving banks were formed under Government Saving Bank Act, 1873.
2. India post payment bank are registered under Companies Act, 2013.

Which of the statements given above is/are correct?

(a) Only 1 (b) Only 2
(c) Both 1 and 2 (d) Neither 1 nor 2

13 **Consider the following statements.**

1. Sukanya Samridhi Scheme focuses on encouraging the parents of girl child for building fund for the education and marriage expenses of her.
2. Mudra Unit development and refinery agency is 100% subsidiary of SBI.

Which of the statements given above is/are correct?

(a) Only 1 (b) Only 2
(c) Both 1 and 2 (d) Neither 1 nor 2

14 **Which of the statements given below are incorrect?**

1. Excise duty is part of GST.
2. FDI involves setting up firms to produce goods and services.
3. The share of direct tax is always more than indirect tax in India.

Codes

(a) 1 and 2 (b) 2 and 3
(c) All of these (d) 1 and 3

15. **Consider the following pairs.**

1. Bretton Wood Conference – IMF
2. International bank for reconstruction and development – World Bank
3. Global economic prospect report – Asian Development Bank
4. New development bank – BRICS

How many of the above pairs is/are correctly matched?

(a) Only one (b) Only two
(c) Only three (d) All four

16 **Consider the following statements with reference to Trade-Related Investment Measure, (TRIMS).**

1. Quantitative restriction on imports by foreign investor are prohibited.
2. They apply to investment measures related to trade in both goods and services.
3. They are not concerned with the regulation of foreign investment.

How many of the statements given above is/are correct?

(a) Only one (b) Only two
(c) All of three (d) None of these

17 **What is/are the purpose of marginal cost of funds based on lending rate?** *(IAS Pre 2016)*

1. These guidelines are used by banks to determine interest rates on loans. Help to increase transparency in the method adopted.
2. These guidelines help in ensuring the availability of bank credit at such rates, which are beneficial for both the borrower and the banks. That is justified.

Select the correct answer using the codes given below.

(a) Only 1 (b) Only 2
(c) Both 1 and 2 (d) Neither 1 nor 2

18 **Consider the following statements about the Indian Capital Market.**

1. Primary market in India is mainly dealt with the new issues and debentures.
2. Primary market in India is supervised by the Insurance Regulatory Development authority.

Select the correct answer using the codes given below.

(a) Only 1 (b) Only 2
(c) Both 1 and 2 (d) Neither 1 nor 2

19 **Which among the following is added to the gross domestic product to arrive at national income of a nation?**

1. Depreciation 2. Subsidies
3. Indirect taxes 4. Net factor income abroad

Codes

(a) Only 2 (b) 1 and 2
(c) 2 and 3 (d) 3 and 4

20 **Which of the following statements is/are incorrect?**

1. KAPILA Programme is launched to increase intellectual property related literacy among people.
2. Global intellectual property index is launched by World Bank.

Codes

(a) Only 1 (b) Only 2
(c) Both 1 and 2 (d) Neither 1 nor 2

21 **Human capital formation as a concept is better explained in terms of a process which enables** *(IAS Pre 2018)*

1. individuals of a country to accumulate more capital.
2. increasing the knowledge, skill levels and capacities of the people of the country.
3. accumulation of tangible wealth.
4. accumulation of intangible wealth.

Which of the statements given above is/are correct?

(a) 1 and 2 (b) Only 2 (c) 2 and 4 (d) 1, 3 and 4

22 **With reference to digital payments, consider the following statements.** *(IAS Pre 2018)*

1. BHIM app allows the user to transfer money to anyone with a UPI-enabled bank account.
2. While a chip-pin debit card has four factors of authentication, BHIM app has only two factors of authentication.

Which of the statements given above is/are correct?

(a) Only 1 (b) Only 2
(c) Both 1 and 2 (d) Neither 1 nor 2

23 **Consider the following statements.**

1. The Fiscal Responsibility and Budget Management (FRBM) Review Committee Report has recommended a debt to GDP ratio of 60% for the general (combined) government by 2023, comprising 40% for the Central Government and 20% for the State Governments.
2. The Central Government has domestic liabilities of 21% of GDP as compared to that of 49% of GDP of the State Governments.
3. As per the Constitution of India, it is mandatory for a State to take the Central Government's consent for raising any loan, if the former owes any outstanding liabilities to the latter.

How many of the statements given above is/are correct?

(a) Only one (b) Only two
(c) All three (d) None of these

24 **Consider the following statements.**

1. Har Khet ko Pani is an initiative under Pradhan Mantri Sinchai Yojana.
2. Neeranchal is a watershed program assisted by World Bank.
3. No chemical fertiliser is used in organic farming.

How many of the statements given above is/are correct?

(a) Only one (b) Only two
(c) All three (d) None of these

25 **Consider the following statements.**

1. Financial intermediaries are entity that acts as the middleman between two parties in a financial transaction.
2. Building societies, hire purchase companies, insurance companies, saving banks, pension funds, investment trusts are example of non-banking financial intermediaries.

Which of the statements given above is/are incorrect?

(a) Only 1 (b) Only 2
(c) Both 1 and 2 (d) Neither 1 nor 2

26 **Consider the following statements.** *(IAS Pre 2017)*

1. National Payments Corporation of India (NPCI) helps in promoting the financial inclusion in the country.
2. NPCI has launched Rupay, a card payment scheme.

Which of the statements given above is/are correct?

(a) Only 1 (b) Only 2
(c) Both 1 and 2 (d) Neither 1 nor 2

27 **Consider the following pairs.**

1.	Delhi-Mumbai Industrial Corridor (DMIC)	– Japan
2.	Chennai-Bengaluru Industrial Corridor (CBIC)	– Japan
3.	Bengaluru-Mumbai Economic Corridor (BMEC)	– World Bank
4.	East Coast Economic Corridor (ECEC)	– Asian Development Bank

How many of the above pairs is/are correctly matched?

(a) Only one (b) Only two
(c) Only three (d) All four

28 **Consider the following statements and choose the correct answer.**

Statement-I Disinvestment in an integral part of Liberalisation of economy in India.

Statement-II The proceeds are being and according to stated policy.

Which one of the following is correct in respect of the above statements?

(a) Both Statement-I and Statement-II are correct and Statement-II is the correct explanation for Statement-I.
(b) Both Statement-I and Statement-II are correct and Statement-II is not the correct explanation for Statement-I.
(c) Statement-I is correct but Statement-II is incorrect.
(d) Statement-I is incorrect but Statement-II is correct.

29 **Consider the following statements.**

1. Special Economic Zones (SEZ) in India are operated by the Ministry of Industries and Public Sector Undertakings.
2. Invest India programme is the official investment promotion and facilitates investments in the country.

Which of the statements given above is/are correct?

(a) Only 1
(b) Both 1 and 2
(c) Only 2
(d) Neither 1 nor 2

30 **Which of the following pairs is not correctly matched?**

(a)	Adma Smith	– Wealth of Nations
(b)	J.M. Keynes	– General Theory of Employment Interest and Money
(c)	Gunnar Myrdal	– Asian Drama
(d)	Karl Marx	– Principles of Political Economy and Taxation

Practice Set 03

1 With reference to the effect of devaluation of a currency, consider the following statements. *(IAS Pre 2021)*

1. Improves the competitiveness of the domestic exports in the foreign markets.
2. Increases the foreign value of domestic currency.
3. Improves the trade balance.

Which of the above statements is/are correct?

(a) Only 1 (b) 1 and 2
(c) Only 3 (d) 2 and 3

2 With reference to mineral resources, which of the following statement/s is/are correct?

1. Lithium's inferred resources have been found in Reasi district of Jammu and Kashmir.
2. India is import dependent for many minerals like lithium, nickel and cobalt. *UPPSC (Pre) 2023*

Select the correct answer using the codes given below.

(a) Only 1 (b) Only 2
(c) Both 1 and 2 (d) Neither 1 nor 2

3 Consider the following statements. *(IAS Pre 2021)*

1. Foreign Currency Convertible Bonds.
2. Foreign institutional investment with certain conditions.
3. Global Depository Receipts (GDR).
4. Non-resident external deposits.

Which of the above can be included in Foreign Direct Investments?

(a) 1, 2 and 3 (b) Only 3
(c) 2 and 4 (d) 1 and 4

4 Consider the following statements.

1. The Reserve Bank of India decides the extent of borrowings permitted to the Government of India.
2. The borrowing programme of the Government of India is administered by the Department of Revenue, Ministry of Finance.

Which of the statements given above is/are correct?

(a) Only 1 (b) Only 2
(c) Both 1 and 2 (d) Neither 1 nor 2

5 It will have the following impact on the economy in reducing the Cash Reserve Ratio (CRR).

1. Banks will have more liquidity advantage.
2. Investment growth can be seen in the economy.
3. Money supply in the economy may increase.
4. Real investment may fall.

How many of the statements given above is/are correct?

(a) Only one (b) Only two
(c) Only three (d) All four

6 Consider the following statements.

1. A capital budget is associated with income and expenditure that are of long term nature.
2. Selling of Public Sector units is an example of revenue receipts.
3. Repo rate is increased by RBI after every budget.

How many of the statements given above is/are correct?

(a) Only one (b) Only two
(c) All three (d) None of these

7 Consider the following statements.

1. The Wholesale Price Index gives more weightage to the primary products because of the dominant role of agriculture in the Indian economy.
2. The Consumer Price Index gives more weightage to manufactured articles on account of change in demand pattern in the economy.

Which of the statements given above is/are correct?

(a) Only 1 (b) Only 2
(c) Both 1 and 2 (d) Neither 1 nor 2

8 Which of the following statements is/are correct?

1. Commercial banks have to compulsorily lend 40% to priority sectors.
2. Startups are included in priority sector lending.
3. Scheduled Commercial Banks are the ones listed in Second Schedule of RBI.

How many of the statements given above is/are correct?

(a) Only one (b) Only two
(c) All three (d) None of these

9 Consider the following statements.

1. Share of agriculture in Gross Domestic Product (GDP) increased enormously.
2. Share of India's exports in Word Trade increased.
3. FDI inflows increased.
4. India's foreign exchange reserve increased enormously.

How many of the statements given above is/are correct?

(a) Only one (b) Only two
(c) Only three (d) All four

10 **Consider the following statements.**

1. MCLR is the minimum interest rate of a bank below, which it cannot lend.
2. Ways and means advances are temporary loan facilities to the Centre and State Governments.

Which of the statements given above is/are correct?

(a) Both 1 and 2
(b) None of the above
(c) Only 2
(d) Only 1

11 **Consider the following statements.**

The 'Stability and Growth Pact' of the European Union is treaty that *IAS (Pre) 2023*

1. limits the levels of the budgetary deficit of the countries of the European Union.
2. makes the countries of the European Union to share their infrastructure facilities.
3. enables the countries of the European Union to share their technologies.

Select the correct answer by using the codes given below.

(a) Only 1 (b) Only 2
(c) Only 3 (d) None of these

12 **Budget deficit may lead to**

1. Rise in the interest rates
2. Fall in value of currency
3. Increase in currency circulation

Which of the statements given above is/are correct?

(a) 1 and 2 (b) 1, 2 and 3
(c) 1 and 3 (d) 2 and 3

13 **Consider the following statements.**

1. India's net exports of goods have a negative balance.
2. India's net export of services have a positive balance.
3. India is the largest receiver of remittances around the world.

How many of the above statements is/are correct?

(a) Only one (b) Only two
(c) All three (d) None of these

14 **Consider the following statements.**

1. Short term debt instruments are usually 'unsecured' because they are not backed by any asset.
2. Masala bonds are rupee dominated bonds released in domestic market.

Which of the statements given above is/are correct?

(a) Only 1 (b) Only 2
(c) Both 1 and 2 (d) None of these

15 **Consider the following pairs.**

1. Fitch – Rating Agency
2. Nationalisation of 14 private sector banks – 1991
3. Basel Norms – Banking
4. Panda Bonds – Chinese Yen Dominated Bonds

How many of the above pairs is/are correctly matched?

(a) Only one (b) Only two
(c) Only three (d) All four

16 **Consider the following statements.**

1. Jan Arogya Yojana is a free health insurance cover upto 2 Lakh for old persons.
2. National Health authority oversees and monitors the implementation of PM-JAY.

Which of the statements given above is/are incorrect?

(a) Only 1 (b) Only 2
(c) All of these (d) None of these

17 **Consider the following statements.**

1. Contractionary fiscal policy involves rising taxes or cutting government spending.
2. Tax cut is a feature of expansionary fiscal policy.
3. Budget is an annual financial statement under Article 110 of Constitution.
4. In 1887, British Indian Government started financial year from 1st April to 31st March.

How many of the statements given above is/are correct?

(a) Only one (b) Only two
(c) Only three (d) All four

18 **Consider the following statements.**

1. Increase in revenue expenditure may lead to inflation.
2. Capital expenditure will not have any impact on employment generation.
3. Interest received on loans is a part of revenue receipts.

How many of the statements given above is/are correct?

(a) Only one (b) Only two
(c) All three (d) None of these

19 **Which of the following statements is/are correct**

1. Nauru is the last country to join World Bank.
2. International Center for Settlement of Investment Disputes (ICSID) works under IMF.

Codes

(a) Only 1 (b) Both 1 and 2
(c) Only 2 (d) None of these

20 **Consider the following pairs.**

1. Trade and Development Report – World Economic Forum
2. Marrakesh Agreement – WTO
3. ILO – Founded in 1939
4. World Economic Situation and Prospects – UNICEF

How many of the above pairs is/are correctly matched?

(a) Only one (b) Only two
(c) Only three (d) All four

21 **Consider the following statements.**

1. World Economic Forum is a non-profitable foundation.
2. Great reset initiative in the post-Covid world is launched by World Economic Forum.
3. India is a member of G7 countries.

How many of the statements given above is/are correct?

(a) Only one (b) Only two
(c) All three (d) None of these

22 **In India, which of the following review the independent regulators in sectors like telecommunications, insurance, electricity, etc?** *(IAS Pre 2019)*

1. Ad Hoc Committees set-up by the Parliament
2. Parliamentary Department Related Standing Committees
3. Finance Commission
4. Financial Sector Legislative Reforms Commission
5. NITI Aayog

Select the correct answer using the codes given below.

(a) 1 and 2 (b) 1, 3 and 4 (c) 3, 4 and 5 (d) 2 and 5

23 **Consider the following statements.**

Statement-I In 1960s, the Government of India under the food and Agriculture Minister Chidambaram Subramaniam launched in Green Revolution with the help of a geneticist, MS Swaminathan.

Statement-II During Green Revolution High-Yielding Varieties (HYVs) of dwarf rice seeds namely Lerma ROTO-64 A and Sonara 64 was introduced in India which were imported from Japan.

Which one of the following is correct in respect of the above statements?

(a) Both Statement-I and Statement-II are correct and Statement-II is the correct explanation for Statement-I.
(b) Both Statement-I and Statement-II are correct and Statement-II is not the correct explanation for Statement-I.
(c) Statement-I is correct but Statement-II is incorrect.
(d) Statement-I is incorrect but Statement-II is correct.

24 **Consider the following statements.**

1. In floating exchange rate, market forces determines the value of domestic currency.
2. Sterlisation by RBI is the process by which RBI takes away access liquidity from banking system to neutralise the fresh money that enter the market.

Which of the statements given above is/are correct?

(a) Only 1 (b) Both 1 and 2
(c) Only 2 (d) Neither 1 nor 2

25 **Which month of the year is celebrated as Rashtriya Poshan maah or National Nutrition Month under the Poshan Abhiyaan of the Government of India ?** *68th BPSC (Pre) 2023*

(a) May
(b) September
(c) July
(d) More than one of these
(e) None of the above

26 **Which of the following statements is/are incorrect?**

1. A micro enterprise is the one in which investment does not exceed 1 cr and turnover not more than 5cr.
2. Udayam Sakhi Portal has been launched for women entrepreneurs.

Codes

(a) Only 1 (b) Both 1 and 2
(c) Only 2 (d) Neither 1 nor 2

27 **Consider the following statements.**

1. Monetary Policy Committee uses WPI data to control inflation.
2. National Statistical Office (NSO) releases WPI.
3. An MBA working in BPO is an example of Disguised unemployment.

How many of the statements given above is/are correct?

(a) Only one (b) Only two
(c) All three (d) None of these

28 **Consider the following statements.**

1. Open Market Operation refers to purchase and sale of government securities by RBI.
2. Call Money market is an interbank money market for short-term financial assets.
3. Market Stabilisation Scheme is a policy tool of RBI to suck excess liquidity from the market.

How many of the statements given above is/are correct?

(a) Only one (b) Only two
(c) All three (d) None of these

29 **Which of the following services are accounted in the Gross Domestic Product of a country?**

1. Services rendered by a domestic help.
2. Services rendered by a worker from unorganised sector.
3. Services produced in Indian embassies located abroad.
4. Services produced in foreign military establishments located in India.

How many of the statements given above is/are correct?

(a) Only one (b) Only two
(c) Only three (d) All four

30 **Which of the following are responsible for the decrease in per capita holding of cultivated land in India?**

1. Low per capita income.
2. Rapid rate of increase in population.
3. Practice of dividing land among the heirs.
4. Use of traditional techniques of ploughing.

How many of the statements given above is/are correct?

(a) Only one
(b) Only two
(c) Only three
(d) All four

Answers

Practice Set 01

1. (c)	2. (d)	3. (b)	4. (b)	5. (b)	6. (c)	7. (b)	8. (c)	9. (b)	10. (c)
11. (c)	12. (a)	13. (a)	14. (b)	15. (d)	16. (b)	17. (c)	18. (a)	19. (c)	20. (c)
21. (a)	22. (a)	23. (b)	24. (b)	25. (b)	26. (b)	27. (c)	28. (c)	29. (d)	30. (a)

Practice Set 02

1. (a)	2. (b)	3. (c)	4. (b)	5. (a)	6. (c)	7. (c)	8. (a)	9. (c)	10. (d)
11. (c)	12. (c)	13. (a)	14. (d)	15. (c)	16. (b)	17. (c)	18. (a)	19. (c)	20. (b)
21. (c)	22. (a)	23. (b)	24. (b)	25. (c)	26. (c)	27. (c)	28. (b)	29. (c)	30. (d)

Practice Set 03

1. (a)	2. (c)	3. (a)	4. (a)	5. (c)	6. (a)	7. (c)	8. (c)	9. (c)	10. (a)
11. (a)	12. (a)	13. (c)	14. (a)	15. (c)	16. (a)	17. (b)	18. (b)	19. (a)	20. (a)
21. (b)	22. (a)	23. (c)	24. (b)	25. (b)	26. (b)	27. (a)	28. (c)	29. (b)	30. (b)